AF491122

BLUE MITTENS

BLUE MITTENS

Coping with my Daughter's Cancer:
A Mother's Memoir

Tracey Ann Webb

Copyright © 2025 by Tracey Ann Webb

All rights reserved.

No part of this publication may be reproduced, distributed, or transmitted in any form or by any means, including photocopying, recording, or other electronic or mechanical methods, without the prior written permission of the author, except in the case of brief quotations used in reviews or scholarly works, or as permitted by U.S. copyright law.

For privacy reasons, most names have been changed.

First edition, 2025

ISBN: 979-8-89694-344-0 - Paperback
ISBN: 979-8-89694-343-3 - eBook
ISBN: 979-8-89694-345-7 - Hardcover

Cover design by Laercio Messias

To my children

Preface

For more than three and a half years, our lives revolved around hospitals, doctors, blood transfusions, and endless finger pricks. A constant cloud of uncertainty hung over us as we faced each day, never knowing what the next would bring.

During that time, none of my friends could fully grasp what my family was enduring—the relentless hope and overwhelming fear, the highs and crushing lows, the small miracles we clung to, and the devastating setbacks we endured. The gap in understanding is part of what led me to write this book. I wanted to share not only my daughter's illness and treatment but also the reactions of those around us, the daily struggles of caring for a sick child, and the alternative therapies we pursued in our desperate search for a cure.

I have written this with complete honesty—uncensored and from the heart—for anyone whose child is facing cancer or another life-threatening disease. I hope these pages bring you some comfort and a sense that you are not alone.

This book is also for those who know a child with cancer but feel uncertain about how to help. Perhaps you don't know what to say or how to act around the family. By reading this, I hope you will better understand what the parents and siblings of that child are experiencing—and how you can offer support and compassion. You may even come to appreciate more deeply your health, your life, and the children in it.

Finally, this is for pediatric doctors, nurses, and caregivers. I hope this book offers a glimpse into the unseen weight carried by the parents accompanying their sick children—their silent grief, relentless vigilance, and unspoken fears.

Throughout my daughter's treatment, friends often said, "I don't know how you cope."

I coped because I had to. There was no other choice.

Contents

Excerpt from a Christmas Letter written on December 12, 1991

Daniela will be two years old on December 18th. She's 35 inches (89 cm) tall and weighs about 27 pounds (12 kg). She is noticeably taller than most other boys and girls her age. She still speaks her own language, but she now uses forty English words and ten German words. Still no two-word sentences, but I assume it will take her longer to talk, since she's learning two languages at the same time. She's at that age where you either have to watch her all the time or else clean up after her, because she's constantly making little messes. In one day, I picked up a pile of leaves she had pulled off of a houseplant, gathered tissues that she had pulled from a box, pinned the papers and pushpins back onto the cork board, put her diapers back where they belong, and put things back into my bottom dresser drawer, not to mention the usual cleaning up of crumbs and spills that happen daily.

In between making messes for Mama and Papa to clean up, Daniela explores and plays independently with her toys and books. Our cat is much more tolerant now, while Daniela pets her and hugs her and offers her a bottle, which the cat thankfully ignores. Often our job as parents is stressful, but the good times far exceed the bad or frustrating times.

Speaking of parenthood, we're expecting our second baby in May. I'm in my 21st week and long over the nausea, but I'm already suffering from backaches, and I still have occasional low blood pressure. We're both looking forward to our new baby, but we naturally fear the unknown changes it will bring into our lives.

Chapter 1

First Symptoms

It all started with a limp.

Daniela was two years and eight months old when I first noticed something was wrong. It was the summer of 1992 during a family vacation in Bavaria to visit my in-laws with my German husband, Joseph. I had taken Daniela out for a walk, pushing three-month-old Alex in a baby carriage, when she struggled to keep up. She was wearing the little red sandals I had bought from a second-hand store—and she was limping.

I immediately blamed myself. Were the shoes too tight? Had I been careless? Guilt gnawed at me as I threw them away that night, convinced they were the cause of her pain.

But the limp didn't go away—and the real cause was far more terrifying than I could have ever imagined.

After our family visit, we drove three hours south to Berchtesgaden to see some friends, an older couple in their seventies. Outside their front door was a breathtaking view of the Bavarian Alps. Whenever we visited them, we went for a daily walk to take in the scenery.

"Hey, Dani," Joseph said, pushing Alex in the stroller. "Do you see the tall mountain on the right?"

"*Ja*," she said.

"That's the Watzmann. The one over there is the Watzmann wife," he continued, pointing to the left. "The small mountains in between—"

"—*sind die Kinder*!" Daniela interrupted enthusiastically.

"That's right, those are the children," he said with a smile.

We also saw the "*Schlafende Hexe*," a mountain shaped like a reclining woman with a long nose.

"Look, Daniela!" I said. "Do you see the sleeping witch? See her big nose?"

"*Ja*, I see it!" she said.

In their early years, our kids spoke a mixture of German (Deutsch) and English: Denglish. Even today, we still slip into it, conveniently choosing whichever word comes to mind first, perpetuating the *Denglish* language.

"That mountain to the left is the witch's breast," I said.

Daniela giggled.

"Alex, *schau*!" she said, pointing to the mountain. Daniela loved sharing things with her baby brother.

While staying with our old friends, Joseph and I slept in the same room with the kids. One night, I was awakened by the sound of Daniela groaning in her sleep, as if she were in pain. I dismissed it as a bad dream.

On our six-hour drive home, Alex slept most of the way, while Daniela groaned again and complained in the car. She had always enjoyed road trips, so this was unlike her.

"I wanna go home."

"We're on our way, Daniela." I reassured her.

"When will we get there?"

"Try to get some sleep, honey. We'll be home soon," I said, hoping to comfort her.

We assumed she was just stir-crazy and eager to get home, like any other kid her age would be. At the time, we had no idea that something was already brewing inside her little body.

The day after returning to our home in Freiburg, nestled in the Black Forest of southwest Germany, I noticed Daniela struggling to ride her tricycle in our apartment. She used both hands to lift her left leg onto the pedal. It seemed unusual.

"Daniela, are you all right?" I asked.

Placing a hand on her hip, her face crumpling into a pitiful expression, she said, "It hurts."

On a whim, I checked her temperature. She had a fever of 102.2°F (39°C).

Since it was a Sunday, we called the *Notarzt*, the emergency doctor. Back then, they still made house calls. When the doctor arrived and examined Daniela, he suspected *Hüftschnupfen*. I had never heard of it before, and the only translation I could find was "irritable hip," which didn't seem to make sense for a child so young. The doctor suggested that to confirm the diagnosis, Daniela would need to have some blood work done.

The next day, I took Daniela to her pediatrician. She still had a fever and wasn't feeling well. In the waiting room, she half-heartedly flipped through a children's book while I read to her. I found it annoying for us to have to wait for up to forty-five minutes, especially in the same room with other children who were sneezing and coughing.

When we were finally called in, the pediatrician examined her thoroughly and with such kindness, that I silently forgave him for having to wait so long. He prescribed pain relievers and took a blood sample to send to the lab. Then he told us that if her fever didn't go away within three days, we needed to take her to the hospital.

The next day we learned that Daniela's C-reactive protein (CRP) was around 6 mg/deciliter—far above the normal levels of less than 0.3 mg/dL. An elevated CRP usually indicates inflammation. Since her fever hadn't subsided, we took her to the University Children's Hospital in Freiburg—called *Kinderklinik*—where she was admitted to *Station Moro*, the hospital ward for infectious disease.

At the end of the wing, a glass door led to a stairwell landing. On the other side was another glass door to *Station Pfaundler*, the children's cancer ward. Through it we could see bald-headed children of all ages pushing intravenous (IV) stands. I felt sorry for them and was glad to be on this side of the glass.

The doctors started Daniela on IV antibiotics, assuming she had osteomyelitis—an inflammation of the bone common in children under the age of five.

For young children like Daniela, the IV needle was inserted into the forearm, taped down, and wrapped in gauze to prevent her from pulling it out. The needle was connected to long tubing attached to a large 50 ml syringe placed in a medical device called a syringe pump, which administered the medication at a precise rate—no guesswork with counting drops per second.

After receiving the IV antibiotics, Daniela's fever went down, but it returned a week later while she was still in the hospital. Since she hadn't responded to treatment, the doctors ruled out osteomyelitis and decided to look for a different cause.

Under sedation, Daniela underwent a small operation to extract a sample of bone marrow. The doctor also aspirated her hip to remove accumulated fluid. When she woke up, her hip pain was gone, and she seemed like her active self again.

The next day, we met with Dr. Zimmermann to discuss the bone marrow results. Edith Zimmermann, head of the

Oncology Department at the Children's Hospital, was a soft-spoken woman, no taller than me, with short, wavy brown hair and wire-framed glasses.

"Are you looking for leukemia?" I asked.

"We've ruled out leukemia," she said.

Joseph let his arm drop next to his body in an exaggerated expression of relief.

I sat frozen, tense with trepidation.

Dr. Zimmermann continued. "We did, however, find some foreign cells—cells that don't belong there."

That didn't sound good. *Isn't that what cancer is? Strange cells that don't belong there?*

"We won't know exactly what we're dealing with until Monday," she said.

Monday! We would have to wait the entire weekend for the histology results.

It was a long, grueling weekend—the first of many to come.

Chapter 2

The Journey to Motherhood

Before I continue with Daniela's story, you might want to know what brought me to Germany. I was born and raised in Miami, Florida, until my family moved to the North Georgia mountains, where I spent my high-school years. After graduating from the University of Georgia, I went to Germany on scholarship at the age of twenty-two. I had the notion of studying the bassoon in a country where many great composers originated: Bach, Beethoven, Handel, Wagner, and Mahler—to name a few. Mozart, who originated from Austria but was German-speaking, composed a bassoon concerto, which became the required piece for orchestral auditions.

My German husband and I first met at the *Hochschule für Musik* (Conservatory of Music) in Freiburg, where I studied for two years. Later, we were both employed by the Police Orchestra in Kiel, a city in Schleswig-Holstein in northern Germany. Eventually, Joseph won a horn audition with the Philharmonic Orchestra in Freiburg. While he began working there at the beginning of March 1989, I stayed on in Kiel.

With an eight-hour train ride separating us, we managed to see each other only about once a month.

By the time we were both twenty-nine, we were ready to start a family. However, when I went to visit Joseph for Easter weekend, I had been counting the days of my menstrual cycle. At day twenty-five, I should have been long past ovulation, so I didn't think I would be able to get pregnant during that visit.

The weather that early spring was warm and dry— perfect for a hike in the Black Forest. I don't remember who thought to take along a picnic blanket or even who initiated it, but we ventured off the footpath into the underbrush and had sex right there in the woods. Hearing hikers passing nearby made the moment even more exciting.

When I returned to Kiel after that weekend, I had no idea that my body—and my life—were already beginning to change.

Good News

Joseph and I decided that I would finish out my year in Kiel and join him around August, which meant we talked a lot on the phone. But when I found out I was pregnant, I wanted to share the good news with him in person.

Joseph had a temporary place to stay in Freiburg but would need to handle the task of finding us an apartment. When he told me about an apartment on the fourth floor of a building without an elevator, I knew that wouldn't work with a baby carriage.

"Joseph, you know I'm a lazy American! There's no way you can get me to walk that many stairs," I said. "You need to find an apartment building with an elevator."

He bought into my argument, never suspecting the real reason behind my insistence.

During my next visit, I finally told Joseph I was expecting.

At first, he was shocked and surprised—just as I had been. Then he shared my excitement and amazement.

"I shouldn't have been able to get pregnant," I told him. "I think because I was away from you, my body was slumbering. Then, when we got together, the egg must have jumped for joy!" (This pun works better in German, since the word for ovulation, *Eisprung*, literally means, "egg jump.")

Whenever I shared my pregnancy news with my German friends, I would make a joke about the egg jumping, and Joseph laughed every time.

While I was still living in Kiel, I went to my first ultrasound appointment alone. As the gynecologist spread gel over my belly, I watched the monitor as it cast images onto the screen.

"I see something," I exclaimed.

"I do, too," the doctor said.

"I see more!" said the doctor's assistant who accompanied us during the ultrasound.

"How many do you want?" the doctor asked. "Two? Three?"

I suddenly understood what I was seeing on the monitor.

All I could say was, "No ... *No!*"

The doctor explained that there were two amniotic sacs, but he couldn't yet detect anything in the second one.

"It might be resorbed by the body, or it could develop into a second embryo," he said.

Since this was my first pregnancy, the thought of having twins felt overwhelming. When I told Joseph about the possibility, he wasn't enthusiastic either. The idea intimidated both of us, but we had to wait four weeks until the next ultrasound to know for sure.

At the follow-up appointment, Joseph was with me. The ultrasound showed that the second sac had dissolved. No twins. I think Joseph was even more relieved than I was.

We got an incredible image of the baby. It was exciting to watch. We could see the profile, a tiny hand raised as if waving at us. It turned to the right, revealing the delicate curve of the spine. Then it pushed off with its tiny feet and swam to the other side. I was captivated. I had no idea babies were so active long before we could feel them move.

German Measles

Just four weeks before I got pregnant, I went to my gynecologist to get a checkup. I told him that we wanted to start a family soon. He took a blood test and found out that I had a negative titer for German measles (also known as rubella). The first rubella vaccines were issued in the mid to late 1960s. Somehow, I must have missed getting vaccinated, since most children receive both doses by the age of six.

I was about seventeen weeks into my pregnancy and could already feel the first movements of my baby, when the mother of one of my young piano students called to tell me that her son had contracted German measles. My mother, who was a nurse, warned me that rubella could cause serious birth defects, such as blindness or deafness in the developing fetus, especially if a woman contracts it during the first three months of pregnancy. My mom, the realist, often painted the bleakest picture.

About ten days after exposure, I woke up one morning to find red splotches all over my chest and back. The rash spread to my neck, face, arms, and legs. Other than the itchiness, I didn't feel sick.

I didn't understand why the gynecologist hadn't given me a vaccine once he discovered I wasn't immune. A subsequent blood test showed that I had developed antibodies for rubella, which weren't present in the first test, confirming that I had gone through the illness.

Perhaps I was far enough along in the pregnancy that I didn't need to worry. Joseph also showed no signs of concern. Either way, we had to wait another five months until our baby was born to know for sure. I soon recovered from the measles, and we both hoped and prayed that our baby would be healthy.

Joseph worked as a musician in the orchestra in Freiburg, while I continued playing the bassoon with the Police Orchestra of Schleswig-Holstein. However, I knew that it was definitely not my dream job. It was a wind ensemble with no strings and lots of brass, so my bassoon playing was often drowned out by the sheer volume of the band. They also played marches and folk music—nothing like the classical music that I loved—and their repertoire hadn't changed in ten years.

In Germany, there are strict laws to protect expectant mothers. One law prohibits women past a certain stage of pregnancy from working after 8:00 p.m. When I reached the five-month mark, this law was about to apply to me. Plus, the pants of my police uniform were getting too tight. However, I wanted to stay through the summer to complete a year with the Police Orchestra. That way, when I quit my job to reunite with Joseph, I would qualify for unemployment.

At the end of August, I gave notice, and we packed and loaded all of our stuff into a rental truck. A girlfriend and I stayed behind to do the final cleaning, while Joseph and my friend's husband drove off with the truck. After we finished cleaning, we returned the apartment key and drove ten hours to Freiburg. About ninety minutes from our destination, we caught up with the rental truck. We all pulled over at the next rest stop and did lots of hugging before continuing the final stretch of the trip.

It was easy to adjust to the city since I had lived in Freiburg before. I spent the rest of my pregnancy in our first-floor, two-bedroom apartment. After Alex, our second child, was born, a three-bedroom apartment became available on the fourth floor. That was our easiest move ever. We used the elevator to transport our furniture, carried our belongings in open boxes, and moved our clothing on hangers.

We had a climbing ivy plant that hung on nails as it spread along the living room wall. Joseph carried the pot while four of our friends held the long stems as they walked up the four flights of stairs, carefully keeping the same tempo to avoid ripping them apart. Now, twenty-five years later, that plant still thrives in my living room.

By the time my thirtieth birthday arrived in November, I was very pregnant, with my due date set for mid-December.

Feelings after Giving Birth

When I went into labor around midnight, Joseph drove me to the hospital, where my contractions continued for over twenty hours, making it impossible to sleep. I wish I could say that Joseph stayed with me throughout the entire ordeal, but at one point, he left the delivery room for a short performance with the Freiburg Philharmonic Orchestra rather than cancel at the last minute. While he was gone, our baby girl was born on December 18th at 8:32 p.m. She weighed 8 pounds and 1 ounce (3660 g) and measured 21-1/4 inches (54 cm) long. Joseph and I had agreed on a girl's name early on. We named her Daniela Marie.

I was amazed by this new life entrusted to me, yet somehow, I had the feeling that she was "on loan." On a spiritual level I felt as if Daniela had been sent to me. I buried that unknown feeling by telling myself that motherhood was simply new and unfamiliar. I wondered if all mothers felt the same way after giving birth.

Years later, I confided in my sister, Lynn, about how I had felt.

"That's funny," she said, "because I always thought that Daniela was supposed to be my child, but she was sent to you."

Lynn, who is two years older than I am, was diagnosed with diabetes at the age of ten. She still reminds me that when I was eight, I was the one who first suggested to our mom that Lynn might have diabetes! (I guess I've always had an interest in medicine.) As an adult, Lynn was encouraged to have children early rather than later. She had two children by the time she was twenty-two, though not without complications, and was advised to use birth control after that.

It amazed me that my feeling of Daniela being lent to me aligned with Lynn's belief that Daniela was meant to be her child. The universe works in strange and mysterious ways.

Milestones

In Germany during the 1980s, new mothers typically stayed in the hospital for a week after giving birth. I arrived home with Daniela on an unusually warm Christmas Day in 1989. I kept an extensive diary about Daniela, perhaps because she was our firstborn child. Most of her milestones were normal, and yet in some ways, she excelled.

At just two days old, Daniela held up her head for over thirty seconds while lying on my chest. By one month, she could prop herself up on her forearms. At five and a half weeks, she warmed us with her first smile. Before she was two months old, she rolled from her tummy to her back. By three months she delighted us with her adorable laugh. I breastfed her and introduced spoon-feeding at four and a half months. Just after five months, she held her own bottle while lying on her back.

By six months, she could sit up on her own for a full fifteen seconds, and a month later, she was crawling and pulling herself up to stand.

At just seven months, Daniela experienced her first flight. Joseph, Daniela, and I visited my family in Georgia. I remember the "bassinet" on the airplane: a cardboard box folded together and placed at our feet for the entire ten-hour flight from Frankfurt to Atlanta. Despite only two hours of sleep in over twenty hours of travel, Daniela arrived cheerful.

My parents doted on their granddaughter during that first visit, and my two nephews, Lynn's sons, aged ten and twelve, were thrilled to finally have a little cousin.

At eight months, Daniela cut her first two bottom teeth. By nine months, she could stand alone for up to fifteen seconds, and shortly before ten months, she took her first steps.

By thirteen months, she was walking independently and climbing onto anything she could—including into the clothes dryer, where she would call out "*Hallo!*" and listen to it echo.

I even caught her on film as she climbed up onto the toilet seat—only to slip and fall off between the toilet and the bathtub. I submitted that video to "*Bitte Lächeln*" ("Please Smile"), a German TV show featuring home videos. It earned Daniela a few seconds of TV fame (not to mention a few *Deutsche Marks* for me).

I suppose all moms like to brag about their children, but I truly felt Daniela was special. Watching her achieve these early milestones filled us with joy and excitement.

Chapter 3

New Diagnosis

On Monday, September 7th, 1992, we met with Dr. Zimmermann. In a calm and professional tone, she told us that Daniela had neuroblastoma. I had worked as a medical records transcriptionist to help pay for college. Since "carcinoma" is the word for cancer, I assumed that any word ending in "-oma" referred to some type of cancer. In Daniela's case, it was the kind that originates in nerve cells— found along the spine and in certain organs. It had already spread to her bone marrow, meaning she had Stage IV neuroblastoma— the most advanced stage with the worst prognosis.

Dr. Zimmermann proceeded to tell us about the therapy Daniela would receive. Chemotherapy—the other big C word. She told us about the risks and that it could cause another malignancy—meaning the treatment itself could trigger a second cancer. What choice did we have but to ignore the possible risks? Of all pediatric cancers, neuroblastoma has one of the lowest survival rates. Even with treatment, Daniela's chances of survival were only twenty percent, a statistic we clung to with desperate hope.

I felt like a bomb had just landed in my lap. I'm sure the doctor told us a lot more, because the conversation lasted for probably twenty minutes, but I looked at her without taking much in. My inner voice covered up most of what she was saying.

My daughter has cancer.

At the end of the conversation, I asked Dr. Zimmermann if she would call my brother-in-law in the United States. My older sister's husband worked as a pediatrician at the CDC (Centers for Disease Control and Prevention) in Atlanta. He would understand the medical jargon and pass on the news to the rest of the family. I couldn't bring myself to do it. When Dr. Zimmermann promised to call him, I surprised myself that I was able to recall his phone number. Joseph and I left in a daze. I didn't even cry. I was just—in shock.

Answering Machine

After a long day at the hospital, I returned home late at night to our apartment, feeling exhausted, numb, and in disbelief. I walked down the narrow hallway to the bedroom but paused at the blinking light of the answering machine and pressed the button.

You have five new messages.

Message one: "Hey!" It was my brother-in-law. "Dr. Zimmermann called me and explained everything. I figured you wanted me to let everyone know. Give us a call."

Message two: "Tracey, it's your Momma." She spoke with a soft but firm voice. "Call me back when you get this."

Message three: "Hi. It's Lynn. I heard the news." My middle sister and I have always been very close. "How are you holding out? I love you. Call me."

Message four: "Hello, Mrs. Webb?" It was the mother of a piano student of mine. "You didn't show up for my daughter's piano lesson today. I just wanted to let you know that she has an appointment with the orthodontist next week."

Oh, crap! I totally forgot about her!

Message five: "Hello Joseph, hello Tracey. Here is Jakob." Joseph's best friend would always start his messages like that, even though we recognized his voice right away. "We're praying for Daniela. The missionaries would like to visit her in the hospital and give her a blessing. Let me know when they can come."

Great, I thought. *Now the whole congregation knows.*

The Church

My parents raised me and my two sisters without religion. My sisters were baptized in Tampa, Florida, where my grandparents lived, but after my parents moved to Miami, they never thought to have me baptized.

When I was thirteen, my family relocated to Blairsville, Georgia— a strong Baptist community. I attended a revival in a Baptist church, was deeply moved by the sermon, and walked to the front of the church to be "saved," yet I didn't feel any real change in my life.

As a teenager, I questioned the purpose of life and what happens after death. When I left home for Converse College in Spartanburg, South Carolina, I was still searching. During my first year there, I met a young man and fell in love. He introduced me to the Mormon Church, officially called the Church of Jesus Christ of Latter-Day Saints, and the missionaries taught me about the faith.

I liked that they didn't baptize children until they were eight years old. I read the New Testament and the Book of Mormon, and I was moved by the story of Joseph Smith finding the golden plates. I had been searching for a missing piece and felt the church filled a void in my life, so in 1979, I was baptized into the Mormon Church. I introduced Joseph to the church shortly after we met.

During the 1990s, when this memoir takes place, the Mormon church was a central part of my life. It provided structure and guidance. It felt like a family away from home. Even though I am no longer a member, I still defend the Mormons whenever I hear someone say anything untruthful about them.

Transfer to the Cancer Ward

While I was at home with Alex, Joseph had to move Daniela from her hospital room, through the two glass doors across the hall, and into Station Pfaundler, the cancer ward. He later told me that he cried while transferring her to her new room. I had never seen him cry before—he tended to bottle up his feelings until they exploded in anger.

Later that day, when I joined him and entered the wing, a sinking feeling washed over me as I saw the many children with thinning or bald hair, their pale faces a stark contrast to the dark circles under their eyes.

All the rooms were single rooms. We were given the first room on the left—the largest in the ward. There was a hospital bed for Daniela and a single bed for me. Apparently, all new patients were assigned this room, and after a few weeks, they were transferred to a smaller room with no extra bed. I assumed they were given the larger room initially to help them acclimate to the new situation of living in the hospital.

I was with Daniela in the hospital room when her pediatrician paid a visit. I felt honored that he came to see us and thought it was so kind of him. He didn't stay long, and I don't remember what he said, but the sympathy he showed during that short visit meant a great deal to me.

At four months of age, Alex was still dependent on my milk, so the three of us lived and slept in the hospital during those first few weeks, with Alex sleeping in his baby carriage. A couple of my well-meaning girlfriends suggested that I wean Alex, but I wanted him to have the same privilege as his older sister. So, I ignored their advice and kept Alex with me. I needed to be there for Daniela, but I couldn't bear to be separated from Alex either.

Broken Tooth

In the summer when Daniela was one and a half years old, we visited our good friends in Denmark, the same friends who helped us with the move to Freiburg. We had met them while attending the Mormon church in Kiel. In fact, their firstborn son, Daniel, was the inspiration for naming our daughter Daniela. We liked the family, and we liked the name.

While we were all shopping at a shoe store, I discovered that Daniela had broken off part of her front tooth. I was so upset that I started to cry. Overwhelmed with emotion, we decided to cut our shopping trip short and return home early.

When I later told these friends about Daniela's cancer, I wrote, "I don't cry over broken teeth anymore."

I must have been a teenager when I saw my mother cry for the first time. It shocked me, because she had always shown strength instead of tears. In her later years, she allowed herself to cry in front of me more often. Yet, I must have inherited her 'stay strong and don't cry' genes, because I believed I had to stay strong for Daniela and hold back my tears.

Mood

When your child has cancer, not all days are bad. I was often in a good mood, because it's my nature to bounce back. When

I attended church and a friend approached me, I was happy to see her and was smiling.

With a solemn and serious expression on her face, she asked me how Daniela was doing.

I found myself converting my smile into a serious face and lowering the tone of my voice to answer her. I felt like I had to mimic her sadness, even though I wasn't feeling particularly down that day. That put a damper on my mood for the rest of the morning at church.

Let this be a hint to those of you approaching your friend who has a child with cancer, or who has cancer themselves. Let them determine the mood—not you! Accept the fact that they can be in a good mood or that they might be having a good day. Don't spoil it for them.

Chapter 4

The Cancer Ward

The day after Daniela was transferred to the cancer ward, I took her to the playroom, where two pre-teen girls with thinning hair sat at a table eating French fries.

The older of the two pointed a fry at Daniela and asked, "Does he want one?"

"She," I corrected her. "This is Daniela."

Undeterred, she asked again, "Does *she* want one?"

While Daniela munched on her French fry, I asked the older girl, "What's your name?"

"Susana. So, what does she have?"

"Neuroblastoma."

She wrinkled her nose. "Is that like leukemia?"

"No, it's a type of malignant tumor."

"Where's the tumor?"

"We don't know yet."

"Oh." Both the girls responded with cautious understanding in their voices.

Susana broke the silence. "I have leukemia."

"Me, too," the other girl added.

I was astounded that they both sounded so matter-of-fact—as if they were saying, "I have a hamster."

"How long have you been here?" I asked them.

"Two months," the nameless girl said.

"I've been here for three months," Susana said, her tone almost bragging.

"How old are you?" I asked Susana.

"Twelve."

"I'm ten," the other girl offered.

After that first exchange, Susana and I would greet each other every day. Whenever I passed her hospital room and the door was open, I heard her calling out a cheerful "*Hallo!*"

"*Hallo, Susana!*" I would always call back in return.

First Block of Chemotherapy

Today, I search the Internet whenever I want to find out about something. Back in the early 1990s, there was no Internet, so I asked the doctors countless questions. I didn't have any idea what chemotherapy really was, how it worked, or how it was administered.

Chemotherapy is a term for powerful drugs that kill fast-growing cells. All kinds of cells. Cancer cells as well as healthy ones. Some have the side effect of causing your hair to fall out, while others might trigger nausea.

Chemotherapy drugs are part of a so-called protocol—a detailed plan for a medical experiment, treatment, or procedure. I guess you could compare a chemotherapy protocol to a computer's operating system. Soon after a new version is released, updates follow. The system is continually tweaked until it is eventually replaced by a new version—which then undergoes its own cycle of updates. Similarly, chemotherapy protocols never seem to have a final version and are constantly evolving.

Chemotherapy drugs aren't administered through a normal vein in the arm the way most IV fluids are. The risk is too high that the aggressive chemo could leak from a vein into surrounding tissue.

Nowadays, a port is surgically inserted under the skin in the chest area and connected to a large vein. From the outside, a needle is pushed through the skin into the port—making it safer and easier to administer the chemotherapy.

However, back in the 1990s, children in the cancer ward had a three-inch tube protruding from their chest called a central venous catheter (CVC), which was connected to a large vein. This meant that the surrounding area was an open wound that had to be cleaned and sterilized regularly.

The end of the three-inch tube connected to a longer IV line, which lead to a bottle hanging from a stand, allowing the medicine to drip slowly for an hour or two. Once the procedure was complete, the nurse sealed the short tube with a red plastic cap, cleaned the wound, dressed it with a fresh bandage, then twisted the tubing onto the bandage and covered it all up with a larger bandage. This had to be repeated weekly, daily, or even more than once a day, depending on the cancer, its protocol, and the prescribed method of treatment.

Today's cancer patients with ports can shower, bathe, and even swim. Back in the 1990s, with a CVC, Daniela couldn't bathe or swim for months. We could only give her sponge baths.

A few days before Daniela's operation to have a CVC inserted, I was curious. Susana, who had gotten her talkativeness from her Spanish mother, didn't seem at all disturbed by the fact that she had to go through chemotherapy, so I thought she wouldn't mind if I asked her about the catheter.

"Could we see your catheter, so it won't be totally strange for Daniela when she gets one?"

"Sure!" Susana said, pulling up her pajama top, exposing both the catheter and her budding breasts. I tried not to show my embarrassment.

"See!" she said, insisting I look. "They put this in so they don't have to stick my arm with a needle all the time. Isn't that great?"

"Wow," I said, stunned. I couldn't believe this pre-teen wasn't shy about showing me her body.

A few minutes later, Susana invited me into her room while the nurse changed the bandage on her catheter. I carried Daniela in and pointed to the tube on Susana's chest.

"See, Daniela? You're going to have one of those, too," I said.

Daniela stared at the CVC with interest but didn't say a word. She also didn't seem fazed by Susana's exposed chest.

Soon after Daniela's chemotherapy began, Susana was discharged. I lost track of her.

I soon learned that never seeing a patient again was usually a good thing.

Mouth Care

Immediately following the surgery to insert the CVC, Daniela began her first round of chemotherapy.

The aggressiveness of the chemotherapy can cause damage to the cells inside the mouth, called oral mucosa, preventing them from fighting off bacteria and leading to painful mouth sores. We were required to perform mouth care with Daniela several times a day. This meant gargling with and swallowing a foul-tasting, rust-colored medicine called Ampho-Moronal. Until it became routine, it was so traumatic for all of us, that I recorded the experience in my journal.

Journal Entry (Fri., Sept. 18, 1992)

I lost my temper tonight. Daniela refused to brush her teeth, clamped her lips shut when I tried to swab her mouth out with Chlorhexamed, and spit out most of the Ampho-Moronal suspension. At first, I was patient with her. Then I pleaded with her. Then I used a threatening tone in my voice. And ultimately, I yelled at her so loud, telling her not to spit, that the nurses came in to see what was going on. It was already past 9:00 p.m., so I probably woke up some of the patients.

"I can't do this!" I told the night nurse, hiding my face with my hands. I felt horrible for losing my patience with Daniela. "You need to do it. You wouldn't yell at her."

She said, "Daniela has to get used to taking her medications and doing her mouth care. Why don't you wait outside while we work with her?"

It has been a fight for the past several days every time Daniela has to take pills or do the mouth cleaning. The nurses assured me that all the children learn how to do it. At this point, I find it hard to believe.

It is so frustrating. The chemotherapy can ruin the mucosa in her mouth, which causes open and painful sores. If that happens, she will have trouble eating. The Ampho-Moronal is to prevent fungal infection of the mouth, stomach, and bowels. I feel so conflicted and hate having to force these meds on Daniela, because she can't stand them, but if I don't do it, she'll suffer even more.

After only two and a half days of chemotherapy, Daniela vomited. Once on Wednesday morning, twice on Thursday evening and twice this morning and once this evening, despite the Zofran, which is given intravenously twice a day for nausea. The night nurse said she doesn't know if Daniela is vomiting because she has an upset stomach, or if it's from the chemotherapy. A lot of children vomit because they've heard that chemotherapy makes you sick, but I think Daniela is too young for it to be psychosomatic.

I'm beginning to think it's not good for Alex to be here with Daniela. When I start to breastfeed him, Daniela stretches her arms out to me and says, "Come 'ere." When other people come to visit, they often pay more attention to Alex, trying to get him to smile or laugh. Tonight, I observed how Daniela looked at the nurses with Alex and didn't look happy.

What should I do? All the books say that siblings of children with cancer tend to feel neglected. If I start weaning Alex from the breast so that other people can take him while I'm with Daniela, then he's being deprived of close contact with his mother. Breast-feeding undoubtedly adds stress to my body, but it's certainly more convenient than warming a bottle.

I breast fed Daniela, started feeding her at 4-1/2 months, and weaned her at 8 months. Alex is so heavy, though, that I am hesitant to give him anything other than mother's milk. Yesterday at the pediatrician's office, Alex weighed 19.1 pounds (8,660 g) and is 26 inches (66 cm) long with a head circumference of 17.3 inches (44 cm). He is four months plus one week old today.

(Note: This put Alex in the 99th percentile for weight, 96th percentile for head circumference, and 78th percentile for height. That means that almost all boys his age weighed less and had a smaller head, and over three-fourths of them were not as long as Alex.)

When Alex gets his first spoonful of food, I want to be there. I also want to observe how he drinks from a bottle. When Joseph has more time to spend with Daniela, I could start weaning Alex slowly. I also want to see how he reacts to different foods.

Hurrah! The first block of chemotherapy medicine was finished around 6 p.m. this evening. Now Daniela is getting "flushed out" with IV fluids over the next three days. She is back down to one IV stand instead of two, which makes walking around much easier.

I asked Dr. Zimmermann when her hair will begin to fall out, and she said usually two to three weeks after the first block of chemo. That's going to be sad. All this time I've been waiting for Daniela's blond curls to get longer. I've only had to cut her hair twice to keep it out of her eyes, but it's still too short and fine to even hold a baby barrette.

Using my journal entries and original faxed letters—all of which I saved—I was able to piece together this memoir. I also went through photo albums and home videos to jog my memory. Some of the stories still bring tears to my eyes, while others make me laugh out loud.

Book Referral

The hospital psychologist lent me a book, which I began reading the night I learned that Daniela had cancer. It was called *Guten Morgen, lieber Tag! Kinder die den Krebs besiegen*, which is the German translation of Erma Bombeck's book entitled *I Want to Grow Hair, I Want to Grow Up, I Want to Go to Boise* (copyright 1989). It took me only twelve days to finish reading it. I often read several books at the same time over several months, so this was fast for me. The book tells the stories of children fighting and surviving cancer and is full of humor and optimism. It helped me get through those first anxious days.

My mother and my older sister, Olivia, are published writers. I've always felt I'd like to write something, but I never knew what it should be. Maybe that's why I kept a journal during Daniela's illness. It certainly gave me something to write about, not to mention that writing everything down helped me sort through my thoughts.

And I hoped that someday Daniela would read it.

Nosy Neighbors

When a neighbor dropped by to ask for my signature on a petition to reduce the speed limit on our street, she kept asking me how Daniela was doing.

Feeling somewhat irritated, I finally said, "She's not doing well at all. She has a malignant disease. It's called neuroblastoma."

"What is that?" she asked.

"It's a type of cancer."

I used the word "cancer" without having to put together that dreaded sentence: *Daniela has cancer.* In fact, whenever anyone asked me what Daniela had, I found it difficult to say *she has cancer.* It was easier for me to say, "Daniela has been transferred to the cancer ward." I tried to avoid having to say more than that.

A ten-year-old girl from the neighborhood who had babysat Daniela saw me as I went out to empty the garbage.

"How's Daniela doing?"

"Not so good, today," I told her. "She has some pain."

"Does Daniela have cancer?"

"Yes."

"Is it true that some people don't survive it?"

"Well, we hope that she will," I said.

Maybe I should have asked her what she knew about cancer. Afterward, I made sure to reassure the children that cancer is not contagious, so they wouldn't be afraid to play with Daniela when she came home from the hospital.

Another time, a singer from my choir called and started asking about Daniela. She had originally called to find out if she could ride to the rehearsal with Joseph, who was subbing for me as the conductor of the choir. I didn't feel like talking to her but couldn't get off the call. In the end, I half-listened while watching ALF play on the TV in the background.

"I've been thinking about Daniela ever since I heard about it—like—all the time," she said.

Although I felt like her words were a bit exaggerated, I politely thanked her for her concern. I knew she meant well, but I found it hard to believe that she had been thinking of Daniela constantly. Even I didn't think of Daniela every minute of the day. If I had, I would have been a wreck, and then I wouldn't have been any help for Daniela.

Some people wanted to know about Daniela because they were genuinely concerned. Others were just curious. It was hard to tell the difference at first. After a while, it became obvious that those who were concerned were the ones who continued to call, visit, or help out.

One day at the hospital, we wanted to take Daniela outside at 3:45 p.m., but the nurse said there was no sense in setting up the portable syringe pump, because her bottle would be empty in an hour, and the IV would be removed from her CVC.

At 4:45 p.m. the IV bottle was empty and one hour later a doctor finally came to remove the IV and seal her catheter. I never understood why a nurse couldn't do it. My mother and two sisters were nurses, so I knew that in the United States, the nurses were allowed to start and run an IV. After waiting for the doctor to come, it was too late to go out for a walk with Daniela. I felt annoyed and disappointed.

Journal Entry by Joseph (Thurs., Sept. 24, 1992)

This journal entry was written by Joseph and was the only time he wrote in my journal.

It's almost 11:00 p.m. Night shift. Daniela has been sleeping since around 9:30 p.m. I'm sitting in the so-called fish room with the huge fish tank, the room where Daniela's illness was revealed to us by the doctors only a few weeks ago, and where we have had several serious discussions with Frau Dr. Zimmermann, the head physician of the Children's Oncology Ward. Today we had another talk. The topic was "intravenous feeding," because Dani's weight has fallen from 28 pounds (12.8 kg) to 25 pounds (11.4 kg) since her admission to the hospital. She has been feeling poorly for days, makes a depressive closed impression, and shows no desire to do anything. During our excursions with the stroller or by bike, she is very quiet and doesn't want to go out or play.

The CT of her head, thorax (chest), and abdomen have revealed nothing new. The search for the primary tumor is now being stopped. I think that the technical diagnostic methods have been exhausted. My first thought is, if there is no large growth (tumor), then there won't be an operation. The chemotherapy and my faith in it must be capable of destroying these malignant cells, although we still have a long way to go. Right now, our major worry is getting Dani to take her meds and being able to do her mouth care, both of which have to be done three times a day. She's slowly beginning to understand or accept it, but it costs us a lot of patience and nerves, and the mouth care usually ends with a "Sauerei"—a huge mess—because she doesn't want to swallow that horrible stuff and thrashes her hands and arms about wildly while she spits it out.

Today is a historical day for me, because a part of my family is coming to visit us for a few days from Bavaria. My sister and her daughter, who is 13 months older than Daniela, and my mother haven't been to Freiburg in a few years, not to mention that my mentally disabled sister has never traveled this far in her life and will be in Freiburg for the first time.

Dani and I used our walk today to surprise everyone at the train station just after their arrival. I'm not sure that was such a good idea, because after greeting Oma, her two aunts, and her cousin, Dani made a sad face when we were separated again. We had to get back to the hospital, and our guests wanted to go to the apartment first to freshen up. We had told Daniela for days who was going to come visit us and often looked at the pictures together from our last trip to my family in Bavaria. My mother and my oldest sister spent the evening with Tracey and Alex, but Dani already felt tired, and it was time for her meds and mouth care. Tonight, she also received a blood transfusion (red blood cells)—she had been looking very pale—and the doctor started her on a liquid diet. At least she didn't have to throw up today. She's been coughing, and I don't like the way it sounds. Tomorrow the doctor is going to listen to her lungs. My hand is hurting from writing. Enough for now, although I still have so many more thoughts in my head. I hope I can remember it all, because every day something new comes along. I'm glad I got my mom to come visit us. It does her some good to get away from home and escape her daily routine.

Joseph's family arrived right after Daniela completed her first round of chemotherapy. I went shopping for groceries with my sister-in-law, and when we returned home, there were delicious smells coming from the kitchen where my mother-in-law was at work. My other sister-in-law was in the living room cleaning windows and the glass table where the plants stood. I felt grateful for all their help.

Daniela had been feeling down prior to their visit, but her cousin managed to get her to laugh. I talked to my mom on the phone, and she told me that laughter is important for Daniela's healing and that we should get her to laugh a lot.

Joseph and his family spent the second day of their visit at Europa Park, while Alex and I stayed in the hospital with Daniela.

I had my first success with Daniela. In the morning, I found a straw on the nightstand, so I crushed Daniela's antibiotic tablets, mixed them with one to two tablespoons of water, and gave the mixture to her in her bear cup with a straw. She sucked it up—not all at once, but with a little encouragement from me. She did it three times that day. I felt so relieved to see some progress.

Daniela also started walking for the first time in several days. She pushed the doll carriage up and down the hall in the hospital ward. Then, with my help, she pushed Alex in the big baby carriage and rode a tricycle. I followed her around, pushing her IV stand and keeping all the IV lines from getting run over or yanked out.

First Signs of Hair Loss (Sun., Sept. 27, 1992)

Daniela was in a good mood and more active. I put Alex in the doll carriage and Daniela pushed him up and down the hall. It was fun to see the nurses' and patients' expressions when they took a second look once they realized the 'doll' was alive!

Daniela was learning new words, and her speech had improved since being in the hospital. She started using German words like *Blut, Pieks, große Spritze, Fieber, Fieber messen,* and *Krankenwagen,* meaning blood, finger prick, big syringe, fever, take my temperature, and ambulance. Not exactly the typical vocabulary for a child less than three years old, but we were excited to hear her talking all the same.

Ten days into chemotherapy, Daniela's temperature rose to 103.5°F (39.6°C), so the doctors started her on antibiotics, which meant she had to be in the hospital for ten days longer.

Her weight dropped to 24.7 pounds (11.2 kg), resulting in a total loss of 3.5 pounds (1.6 kg) during her stay in the hospital. This 12.5% loss of her body weight prompted the doctors to start feeding her intravenously to prevent further weight loss. The proteins and carbohydrates came in a bag of clear fluid, while the fats were in a large 50ml syringe that were slowly injected into the central venous catheter by a syringe pump. The fatty substance was a milky white. Daniela called it "milk" and must have thought we were pumping milk into her veins.

While Joseph's family visited us, his mother celebrated her fifty-seventh birthday. She baked us apple strudel for lunch and a cake for later. I ate first and then drove to the clinic to relieve Joseph.

When I arrived, Joseph told me that Daniela's hair was already starting to fall out. We had been told this would happen two to three weeks after beginning chemotherapy; the next day would mark two weeks. I had hoped it would take longer before her hair began to fall out. Running my fingers through Daniela's hair, I found four or five strands of hair in my hand. There were several more in her new cap, which she must have worn that morning.

As time passed and more hair fell out, I decided to cut off a lock of Daniela's hair and save it before it became too thin. I figured when her hair grew back, I could compare the color to see if it had gotten any darker.

Daniela started to look better and, thanks to the antibiotics and intravenous feeding, seemed to feel better, too. She didn't even look sick anymore, so when she began to lose her hair, it was real blow to us. Her baldness would become a constant reminder that she had a serious illness.

Daniela started eating more and was obviously feeling better, much to my relief. She benefited from a second transfusion of red blood cells, a transfusion of blood platelets, and a round of antibiotics, which helped her fever to go down.

She stopped using the toilet when she was first hospitalized and had to wear diapers again. After the first month of chemotherapy, Daniela opened the closet door and saw her pink plastic potty.

"Pee pee," she said.

"Do you wanna do pee pee?" I asked.

"*Ja.*"

She put more pee in that potty than she ever had before. She even used it a second time that day. Who knew I could feel so grateful for a child performing such a simple everyday task?

I finished writing a letter to Marilyn, a dear friend of mine from Australia, whom I had met at church in Nürnberg and who had moved near Salt Lake City. We had visited Marilyn and her husband in Utah the previous summer with Daniela, a few weeks before their first child was born.

Our thoughts must have crossed, because about two hours later I got a phone call from her. Marilyn said she couldn't sleep since 5:15 a.m. in Utah.

When I told her the horrifying news about Daniela's cancer, she cried.

While trying to regain control of her voice, she said, "I'm sorry, I'm crying."

"That's all right. That's all I did the first few days, but I've told this story so many times that I'm all cried out."

"I can imagine," she said.

I was touched that Marilyn shed tears at the news of Daniela's illness.

A woman from church also cried. She and her daughters often babysat Daniela. They all adored Daniela, and she liked them, too.

Chapter 5

Other Families

At the Children's Hospital, we were not only faced with our child's illness, but we were also exposed to the struggles of other families and their children. Somehow, I had this odd notion that my daughter would be the last child to become ill with cancer. I was shaken back to reality as new families arrived with their own sick children.

On September 25, 1992, Joseph and I attended our first support-group meeting for parents of children with cancer. We were grateful to be able to attend a meeting where we could talk about our challenges with our daughter's illness or treatment, and the others could relate. The meeting was organized by the Children's Hospital. Parents attending the meeting had a child who was either at the beginning of therapy or already in remission.

I met a woman whose daughter had a Wilms tumor, a type of childhood cancer that originates in the kidney. Her daughter was 17 months old when they found blood in her diaper and had been admitted to the hospital three days before

I met them. The night preceding the meeting, the mother had found out the diagnosis and was still close to tears.

My chest tightened as I felt her desperation.

Down Syndrome and Leukemia

There is a huge difference between children and older people who are diagnosed with cancer. The elderly have lived a long life, and many of them already realize they don't have much time left. A cancer diagnosis may give them a chance to get things in order before they pass. Children have a whole life ahead of them. They still have so much to learn and to look forward to. If only they didn't have cancer.

If I wanted to forget about my own troubles, all I had to do was look around the cancer ward to find someone who had an even heavier cross to bear.

There was a 16-month-old girl with Down syndrome and a heart defect who was admitted to the Children's Hospital with leukemia. My first thought was that with a heart defect, she might not be able to withstand the chemotherapy.

Then my next thought was, *Why put her through chemotherapy at all?* I felt bad for even thinking that. What a difficult decision that must have been for her parents.

As it turns out, I never saw her in the cancer ward again.

Family with Five Children

During almost four years of treatment, we learned of several patient deaths from the oncology ward. Very few children succumbed to the cancer itself. Instead, many became so weakened by the chemotherapy that a common cold could overwhelm their already fragile immune systems. What began as a simple cold could escalate into pneumonia and ultimately claim their lives.

One of the first people we met at the Children's Hospital in Freiburg was Martin. He was the father of five children and seemed to spend more time at the hospital than his wife—or maybe he simply talked to us more than she did. Martin was a soft-spoken, kind man from the countryside who traveled long distances to the hospital. He told us that his youngest daughter was in remission at the age of three following treatment for leukemia, when his 13-year-old daughter was also diagnosed with leukemia. I couldn't believe it—two cases of leukemia within one family! During the course of Daniela's treatment, the older daughter was cured of her leukemia, but his youngest suffered a relapse and eventually died. She was one of several who had a weakened immune system from the chemotherapy and succumbed to pneumonia.

My heart ached for that family.

Years later, Joseph ran into Martin in town. He told Joseph that the older daughter had just completed trade school when she suffered a relapse of leukemia. She passed away at the age of twenty.

Somehow the world seems so unfair when young people have to suffer so much—and their families along with them.

Russian Girl in a Wheelchair

In the cancer ward, we encountered a pretty seven-year-old Russian girl with long blond hair and a quiet personality. Her family brought her from Russia to Germany specifically for treatment. She had neuroblastoma like Daniela, but her tumor had grown along the spine, leaving her permanently disabled.

She sat in a wheelchair and could push the wheels herself to get around. She attended the School for the Disabled in the town of Wasser near Emmendingen. The last I knew, this young girl had been released as cured—but she would always rely on a wheelchair for mobility.

Chapter 6

Healers

Joseph studied horn at the *Musikhochschule* (conservatory of music) in Freiburg with a renowned horn professor from England. His teacher was not only an exceptional horn player but also a jolly, humorous man with unexpected talents—one of which was spiritual healing.

When the horn professor learned about Daniela's cancer, he offered to do some healing sessions with her. We were open to the idea. When he visited Daniela, he brought her a small wire tree with tiny gemstone leaves. (Sadly, that tree disappeared from Daniela's hospital room within a few days. It was disheartening to think that someone would steal from a child's room in the cancer ward!) Once the horn professor finished his session, he put us in touch with his friend, Angelina, who had taught him healing techniques.

Angelina—who was an English-speaking Canadian, a flutist, and about my age—called me the next morning. She wanted to know more details about Daniela and asked if she should come over. I told her I'd be grateful if she would have a look at Daniela and place her healing hands on her.

She first visited Daniela in the hospital two or three weeks into therapy. Angelina was a slender, soft-spoken woman with long brown curly hair and radiant blue eyes. Whenever we greeted each other, she first traced the outline of my body with her eyes.

One day, I asked her, "Can you see auras?"

"Yes, I can." She looked slightly sheepish as she answered.

I thought that was amazing. She told me she had this gift ever since she was a child.

She was a kind soul who not only treated Daniela but also occasionally strengthened me with her hands if she saw that I needed it. When Daniela wasn't in the hospital, I took her to Angelina's home, or Angelina came to ours. Since it was about a thirty-minute drive, Angelina and I would often opt to talk on the phone. She could envision things and tell me how Daniela was doing or what her spiritual guide was telling her. Although she made her living as a healer, she never accepted money for treating Daniela, saying that she always treated children for free.

Charlatans

During this time, Joseph and I happened to watch a healer featured on German television. We were open to any healing possibilities for Daniela, so Joseph wrote a detailed letter explaining her illness and asking for help.

We received a generic form letter in return, explaining that so many people had contacted him he couldn't possibly help everyone. Instead, he offered to sell us a video. As parents of a sick child, we were willing to try anything, so we ordered the video for, I believe, 25 German Marks and watched it. The video was nothing more than a documentary of the healer's successes, glorifying his work. It offered no actual help for our daughter.

I remember feeling both scammed and robbed of not just our money, but also our hope. Above all, I felt let down. Someone had taken advantage of our desperate situation and yet offered nothing tangible to help.

Journal Entry (Sat., Oct. 10, 1992)

I haven't written much because I've been so tired that I couldn't keep my eyes open when I went to lie down at night. Daniela was unexpectedly released this past Thursday. Her blood count is still low, but it's on the rise, and she's in good spirits—and they unfortunately need the space in the hospital. Joseph told me that there were five patients in a four-bed room. Two children and their parents were all sitting on one bed waiting for a vacancy.

Daniela was so excited to go home. The first thing she did was to look for Dessa, our cat. She looked in the living room and then in her bedroom, where she discovered the crib that we had set up for Alex.

"Daniela's Bett," she said.

"No, that's Alex's bed." Pointing to her bed, I said, "This is Daniela's bed."

A new doll that I had picked out for Daniela and placed on her pillow caught Daniela's sight immediately.

"Puppe!" she squealed in delight.

She had already forgotten that the crib was for Alex.

Later, though, she climbed into the crib and covered herself with the blanket and played with the baby mobile hanging from above. At night, there was no problem putting her in her bed and Alex in the crib.

Daniela didn't want to take a nap. She had to go through her toys and ride her bike. It wasn't until we took a ride in the car to pick up her medicine from the drugstore that she fell asleep from the vibrations of the car.

Today we were in the Old Town for the first time in ages. I bought some pajamas for Daniela and Alex and a pair of blue mittens with a matching cap and scarf for Daniela. We all ate dinner together at Wiener Wald, and Daniela ate more than she has in weeks and was well-behaved.

She's in such a good mood now that I can't face the idea of putting her back into the hospital. The next block of therapy begins Monday and will make her feel bad again.

Journal Entry (Tues., Oct. 20, 1992)

On Monday, October 12th, Daniela had a rash that looked like measles, so they sent her back home to get over it instead of admitting her for the second block of therapy. On Thursday, October 15th, we took Daniela back to the hospital for another blood test and possible readmittance. Since she only had about 500 granulocytes, they sent her home until Monday. They'd like for her to have at least 800 before starting the next block of therapy.

I often wrote the word "therapy" in my journal, because I didn't like to write "chemotherapy" or "chemo," with all their negative connotations. The word "therapy" sounded better to me, as if suggesting a more positive outcome.

Chapter 7

In Search of the Primary Tumor

Since the neuroblastoma, or cancer cells, had spread to the bone marrow, the primary tumor had to be found. Over four months, from September 1992 to January 1993, Daniela underwent numerous examinations to locate it.

During this time, I became acquainted with X-rays, ultrasounds, computer tomography (CT), bone scintigrams, and magnetic resonance imaging (MRI). Since my mother and both my sisters were nurses, I was often exposed to stories from their workday over dinner. This sparked my interest in medicine, and I was fascinated by the various diagnostic procedures as I accompanied Daniela throughout each one.

When she had to undergo an MRI, the doctor gave her something to help her sleep. Unlike X-rays or CT scans, an MRI does not involve radiation. Instead, the images of the organs are captured using various magnetic fields and radio pulses. When the scanner takes these images, it emits loud buzzing or pounding sounds that may frighten children, which is why sedation is often used for the procedure.

Before entering the room with the MRI scanner, I was told to remove all items containing metal, such as keys, coins, jewelry, a watch, and eyeglasses. Wallets and purses had to be left in the console room because the strength of the magnet would erase all the data from credit cards. I obediently took off my necklace and earrings and placed them in a cardboard emesis basin—the kidney-shaped bowl used by patients who need to vomit.

I carried Daniela from the stretcher to the MRI table while a nurse held the IV bottle. As I neared the round opening of the scanner, I felt something pull at my hair. At first, I thought the IV tube had tangled in my hair as the nurse walked past me to hang up the IV bottle on a non-metallic stand. I took a step back, and the tugging stopped. When I moved forward again, my hair was pulled once more. Then it hit me—I had a metal barrette in my long hair, and the strong magnetic field was pulling at it. I hurried back to the console room and added the barrette to my other belongings. (Joseph later told me he had a similar experience when the buckles on his Birkenstock sandals were pulled by the magnetic force during another MRI with Daniela.)

The medical technical assistant placed Daniela on the flat patient table and placed a so-called radiofrequency (RF) coil around her abdomen. This coil would capture and transmit the images to the computer. At this point, I had to leave the room, but I was able to watch from the console room. MRI scans take significantly longer than other imaging procedures, anywhere from twenty to fifty minutes, depending on the sequences used.

I watched the computer monitor as the images appeared. I was unable to decipher the shifting patterns of black, white, and gray.

I don't recall which procedure ultimately revealed the tumor's location. I only remember it took the doctors until January to determine that the primary tumor was in the left adrenal gland. The tumor had taken up the size and space of the adrenal gland, making it difficult to detect. Needless to say, both Joseph and I were relieved that the primary tumor had finally been found, even if it meant surgery was inevitable.

We approached Daniela's surgery with hopes of a positive outcome. The surgeons removed her left adrenal gland, leaving a long scar on her belly. Daniela recovered quickly from anesthesia and bounced back to her usual cheerful self.

Following surgery, the standard procedure was to send off the tissues for a histology report. The report showed that even after four months of chemotherapy, active cancer cells still remained in the tumor.

That didn't sound good.

Daniela had numerous stays at the hospital. One of the rooms she stayed in had a window to the next patient's room, separated by a curtain on the other side. Sometimes, the small girl in the neighboring room would crawl under this curtain, prompting Daniela to make silly faces at her. Her antics always made people laugh, especially Alex.

Radiation Treatment (June 16 to July 8, 1993)

During the summer of 1993, Daniela had to undergo radiation therapy. By then, she was three and a half years old. At her first appointment, the machines had to be set up specifically for her. The radiologist took a black permanent marker and drew a rectangle on the left side of her belly, stretching from below her rib cage to her abdomen. These markings were used to line up the machine to ensure the same area was radiated each time, so we weren't allowed to wash them off.

I took Daniela's baby doll with us to keep her company, laying it on her legs while she underwent the radiation. I couldn't help but notice that the baby doll's bald head matched Daniela's.

I have several pictures of Daniela with no hair. In each one, she is smiling and looks happy. She doesn't seem embarrassed or ashamed of her baldness. I, on the other hand, felt uncomfortable, because I sensed the discomfort it brought to other people who saw her.

Since I had to take Daniela for radiation treatment every day for three weeks, we made a ritual of it. Aaron, another child with neuroblastoma, became part of this routine. He was a year younger and much smaller than Daniela. The two became friends instantly, so his mom and I took them together.

We pushed our children in strollers from the Kinderklinik to the main hospital for the radiation therapy, which took place in the *Medizinische Klinik*, the Department of Internal Medicine. Since it was summer, after each session, I bought us some ice cream.

It got to be expensive buying ice cream every day at the newsstand, so I went to a large discount store and bought a box of 24 orange popsicles. I found them more refreshing than ice cream. Each morning before therapy, I packed four popsicles into a small, insulated bag—one for Daniela, one for me, and two for Aaron and his mom.

We sat on a bench while the kids remained in their strollers, watching the ducks in the pond as we enjoyed our popsicles. Daniela loved looking at the flowers carefully planted throughout the hospital's park. Her favorites were yellow ones, especially large tulips.

Statistics and Chance of Survival

There's something funny about statistics. I never spoke of it to other parents of children with cancer, but we knew from the start that Daniela only had a twenty percent chance of surviving. Throughout Daniela's illness, we strongly hoped and believed she would belong to that twenty percent. That being said, every time another child died, I was distraught and discouraged. Yet, secretly, I felt that every death meant that my child moved closer to belonging to that small group of survivors. This kind of thinking helped me to maintain hope for my child.

Chemotherapy Can Kill Too Many Cells

During chemotherapy, the doctors had to closely monitor the patient's blood count. While the chemo kills cancerous cells, it also kills healthy blood cells, causing the patient's blood count to drop. Daniela and other young cancer patients often received blood transfusions in the days following their chemotherapy sessions.

Until my experience with Daniela in the hospital, I didn't realize that patients don't receive whole blood. Since the 1990s, donated blood has been separated into its components. Red blood cells are responsible for transporting oxygen throughout the body. When the hemoglobin or red blood cell count drops too low, a patient becomes anemic and weak, requiring a transfusion of "erys," short for erythrocytes. A plastic transfusion bag full of erys appears dark red, so one might assume the patient is receiving whole blood, but that isn't the case.

Thrombocytes, or "thrombos" as they were called around the kids, are platelets responsible for blood clotting. Since the effects of the chemotherapy aren't immediate, it can take a few days for platelet levels to drop. Anyone with a platelet count below 50,000 is at serious risk for internal bleeding. During chemotherapy, children's platelet counts often plummeted below 10,000 before they received a platelet transfusion. This part of the blood is yellow, so we always knew when a child was receiving platelets—the transfusion bag contained yellowish fluid instead of red.

A patient named Sabrina was between phases of chemotherapy, which meant she had to go to the hospital regularly for checkups and blood transfusions. Because she lived with her parents in Constance, a two-hour drive to the Children's Hospital in Freiburg, her parents frequently took her to a local doctor to have her blood count checked.

One day, shortly after a chemotherapy session, Sabrina's platelet count dropped dangerously low. Before the ambulance could get her to Freiburg for a transfusion, she suffered a brain hemorrhage. Sabrina died in March 1996. She was six years and nine months old.

I remember feeling shocked at this news. Sabrina hadn't succumbed to cancer itself, but to the side effects of the chemotherapy.

This stirred up a heated discussion between Joseph and me. He felt Daniela was receiving too much chemotherapy. I felt we had to trust the doctors and their protocols. I wanted Daniela to undergo whatever treatment was necessary to give her the best chance of survival.

Chapter 8

Hot Dogs, Smoke Alarms, and Firemen

On the old *Pfaundler* wing, a closet had been converted into a tiny kitchen to provide parents with a place to prepare their meals. One day, I was frying hot dogs in some oil. There was neither an exhaust fan nor a window in the room.

When I walked out of the kitchen, I noticed that the large glass doors at the end of the hall were closed. They were never closed, so I thought that was odd.

The next thing I knew, one of the nurses came rushing onto the floor.

"Where's the fire?"

"What fire?" I asked.

"The fire alarm was set off," she said. "The firemen are on their way!"

"Oh, no!" I said. "I was only frying hot dogs. Can you call them off?"

"No, I can't," she said and explained that the alarm didn't ring on the hospital ward. Instead, it lit up at the main reception desk and rang directly at the fire station.

Only a few minutes later, some firemen arrived on the floor. After we assured them there was no actual fire, they used the opportunity to visit Daniela, Alex, and other children in the ward.

Both Daniela and Alex were thrilled to see real firemen, complete with their protective gear and helmets.

"Do you have a ladder?" Daniela asked one of them.

"Well, now, let me see," the fireman said, pulling out his two-way radio to speak to a colleague on the other end. "One-four-two, this is eight-six-one. Do we have a ladder on the truck? Over." His eyes shifted between Alex and Daniela as he stifled a grin.

"Affirmative. Over," came the crackly voice.

"Roger, over." The fireman turned to Daniela, "Yes, we have a ladder with us."

The kids were impressed and beamed with pleasure.

I was relieved that my mishap had turned into a memorable experience for Daniela and Alex.

The next time we returned to the hospital, a new sign had been posted in the parents' kitchen that read something to the effect of: *Anyone who causes the fire department to respond to a false alarm will be responsible for the costs.* I was told it would be about four hundred German Marks!

Only a few days later, I was frying hot dogs again. When I stepped into the hallway, I saw the glass doors swing shut. Panic set in as I noticed a wisp of smoke drift toward the ceiling. I didn't want to be stuck with a hefty bill for a false alarm! I rushed over to the nurse's station.

"Please cancel the fire department! There's no fire. It was just me in the kitchen again!"

This time we were able to stop them from coming. Boy, was I relieved! That would have been a very expensive hot dog dinner.

Europa Park

Between treatments, we managed to squeeze in a day at Europa Park in late April 1993 and again in July. I used to think Europa Park was a cheap version of Disney World, but it has grown into one of the top amusement parks in Europe, even competing with Disneyland Paris. Situated in the small town of Rust, Germany, the residents receive a free annual pass to Europa Park as compensation for the thousands of cars that drive through their town. We had to drive only half an hour from Freiburg, making it easy to visit the park on a day trip.

Because I am prone to motion sickness and can't handle rides that move in circles, I was the designated photographer, while Joseph took the kids on the rides I wanted to avoid. Daniela loved the dizzying cup and saucer ride, and both kids screamed with joy when the Tyrolean log flume crested the hill and sped down the slope, splashing at the bottom. We all enjoyed gliding and bumping along the rapids of the Fjord Rafting ride. The kids found it even more fun whenever they got wet.

I think the kids' favorite attraction must have been the "*Rittershow*," where knights dressed in armor rode decorated horses. With expertly timed choreography, they performed a competition featuring duels with realistic-looking lances, swords, and shields.

I cherished being able to spend a fun day with my family without having to worry about doctor appointments or blood transfusions.

Alex's First Birthday

Daniela was in the hospital for another round of chemotherapy when Alex turned one year old. Since we were often at the hospital, we hired an American woman named Doris to help with housework. Over time, she became a friend, so I invited her to Alex's birthday. She asked me if she should bring a cake. I said that would be great.

Doris brought a homemade cake shaped like a cat with pointed ears, M&M eyes, and a single candle for the belly button. Joseph, Daniela, Doris, and I celebrated with Alex in the hospital, joined by some of the children from the cancer ward.

Afterward, Doris said, "I can't believe you didn't bake Alex a cake."

"What do you mean?" I asked.

"What would you have done if I hadn't baked a cake?"

"You told me you were going to bake a cake. I figured one cake was enough."

One cake *had* been enough. I was with Daniela and Alex in the hospital—when could I have possibly baked a cake? Besides, a first birthday is more for the parents than for the child. Still, Doris had managed to make me feel guilty, no matter how I looked at it.

Some friend she turned out to be.

Chickenpox

In the summer of 1993, several cases of chickenpox were going around. The doctors warned us that because of Daniela's suppressed immune system from chemotherapy, she would need to be hospitalized if she contracted the disease.

A friend of ours had a birthday party for her son at church. She invited Daniela, Alex, and a bunch of children from the congregation. We were glad that Daniela was feeling well enough to attend, so we went. The kids had a good time.

A couple of days later, this same friend called to warn me that one of the boys at the party had come down with chickenpox, which meant he had been contagious during the party.

Sure enough, about a week later, Daniela and Alex woke up one morning with the typical pink bumps. Daniela developed blisters all over her body and had to be hospitalized for treatment with special medicine. Alex didn't have as many blisters.

After that episode, we avoided taking Daniela to any place where large crowds gathered. That meant no church, no kindergarten, and no public transportation like buses or trams, where sick people cough their germs into the air. One of the worst things about chemotherapy was having to stay away from friends. While Daniela had her little brother and Joseph still had his work, I felt increasingly isolated at home.

Farewell Party (Thurs., July 8, 1993)

Once all the surgeries, chemotherapy, and radiation treatments were completed according to protocol, the last step was a minor surgery to remove the CVC. Then, the child was released from the Children's Hospital with a small farewell party thrown by the nurses and other patients in the children's cancer ward.

In July 1993, after almost a year of treatment, Daniela was released at three years and seven months of age—with peach fuzz for hair. We celebrated at home with Daniela taking a bubble bath in the bathtub. She could finally enjoy swimming again, since she no longer had a tube protruding from her chest. It was perfect timing for the hot summer months.

That summer, we visited my in-laws in Bavaria, where Daniela played with her cousin. At a folk festival in town, she and Alex rode together on the children's carousel, choosing to sit in the little firetruck—of course. In August, we even attended a wedding, and Daniela danced cheerfully with her friends from church. Her life was finally filled with normal kids' stuff.

Life felt good again.

Chapter 9

Family Rehab in Bad Oexen

Joseph and I were usually exhausted, so we often lacked the energy or desire to make love. One late night, he insisted on having sex. We used a condom and fell asleep right away. I always went to the bathroom after sex, but I was too tired for even that. The next morning, I found the used condom still inside me. I was fuming. Why hadn't he removed the condom when he pulled out?

I had been breastfeeding Alex and didn't menstruate until he was about four months old, which was shortly before the condom incident. When my period didn't come soon after that, I assumed it was because my cycle wasn't regular yet.

One day, I felt a sharp pain that radiated down to my tailbone. It subsided within a few seconds. I thought it was odd but brushed it off. About two weeks before we were planning to go to a family rehab clinic, I felt another painful sensation in my pelvis.

Since my period was overdue, I wanted a doctor's appointment right away. I knew I wouldn't get one unless it was an emergency. So, I called the doctor, explaining my pain and claiming I feared a tubal pregnancy.

It worked. I got an appointment that day.

The doctor did a pregnancy test and informed me that it was positive.

When he saw my dismay, he stated, "So, you're not happy about this."

"No," I replied.

Alex was fourteen months old, and Daniela still had ongoing doctor appointments.

I told him there was no way my body or mind could handle another pregnancy or child at that time.

"Do you want to terminate the pregnancy?"

I nodded in silence.

He gave me the address of a doctor in Karlsruhe, and I got an appointment within a week.

We asked the child psychologist, who had been working with Daniela, to look after both kids. We didn't look for a babysitter at church. We were taught that abortion was wrong, but I strongly believed some situations justified it. After two stressful years and the uncertainty of Daniela's health—not to mention that Alex was still in diapers—I knew I couldn't handle another baby. With Daniela needing most of our attention, bringing another child into our lives wouldn't have been fair to Alex either.

Joseph agreed with me. We drove ninety minutes to Karlsruhe for the procedure. When the doctor began the ultrasound, I looked away. I didn't want to see anything resembling an embryo. They sedated me, and the procedure didn't take long.

An abortion can be performed either by vacuum aspiration, which uses gentle suction to clear out the uterus, or by dilation and evacuation (D&E), which uses medical tools to remove tissue. I usually wanted to know the details of a medical procedure, but in this case, I didn't. I just wanted to get it done.

A week later, on August 18, 1993, we left for our four-week family rehab in the *Kinderhaus Bad Oexen*, an oncological rehabilitation center for children and their families in Bad Oeynhausen. The timing wasn't ideal. The doctor told me I couldn't swim for at least a week.

A day after we arrived, we gathered with all the families in a large circle. While everyone was still introducing themselves, I felt a sharp pain radiating into my back. It was so bad that I almost fainted.

I saw one of the doctors at the rehab center and felt the need to tell him about my abortion. He suspected an infection in my uterus and sent me to the hospital. This triggered guilty feelings, as if I were being punished.

The doctors at the hospital assumed the abortion had been incomplete, so they performed a D&C (dilation and curettage), another uterine scraping under general anesthesia. But before the end of the week, the pain returned.

That day, a young, inexperienced doctor did the rounds. I told him about the sharp, recurring pain. He performed an ultrasound but saw nothing unusual.

When the pain persisted the next day, I said, "This isn't normal. There's something wrong with me. It feels like the pain is around my kidneys. You need to look for something else."

The young doctor must have thought I was exaggerating because he dismissed my concerns.

Shortly before lunch, the head physician did his rounds and took me seriously. He ushered me into his office for a transvaginal ultrasound, the same procedure the young doctor had performed.

After a few moments of examination, he asked, "When did you last eat?"

"At eight o'clock this morning," I said.

"Don't eat or drink anything else. You need to go to surgery."

At 2:00 p.m., I lay on the operating table.

It turned out I had a tubal pregnancy. The pregnancy was already twelve weeks along. If it had continued much longer, my fallopian tube could have ruptured, causing life-threatening internal bleeding. I was relieved to know that I hadn't had a true abortion after all. The guilt lifted, yet I kept this secret— until writing it in this memoir.

I was in the hospital for three of the four weeks while Joseph spent time with Daniela and Alex at rehab. I experienced most of the rehab only through the pictures that Joseph took. It looked like they had a wonderful time. Both kids went horseback riding and played in an adventure playground. Alex was able to attend daycare, while Daniela had swimming lessons and even went on a children's tour of a small underground mine, where she was outfitted with a royal blue coat and a bright yellow, child-sized helmet. The children also had opportunities to finger paint, tie-dye, and do other crafts. They even attended a concert with the spa orchestra, which I imagine Joseph enjoyed the most.

I missed out on all that. I felt robbed of our family rehab. I also felt resentment toward Joseph, because his carelessness had put me in this situation. The doctors wanted to keep me in the hospital longer, but I asked to be released a couple of days before we had to return to Freiburg.

Chapter 10

Blue Mittens

After Daniela completed her chemotherapy, we were able to experience some semblance of normalcy. Daniela celebrated her fourth birthday at home with a couple of my close girlfriends and their children. A week later, we celebrated Christmas with lots of presents under the artificial Christmas tree.

Germans usually buy a real tree and put it up on Christmas Eve. I prefer to decorate for Christmas three to four weeks in advance, so it makes sense for me to use a fake tree that won't shed its needles by Christmas. That year, two large stuffed reindeer sat in front of the tree, since they didn't fit beneath it.

In the winter, Daniela was on maintenance therapy and had to go to the Children's Hospital for regular checkups. Daniela and Alex celebrated *Fasching* both in the hospital and at church. The terms "Fasching," "Fasnacht," and "Karneval" are used in different parts of Germany to describe a festival that occurs seven weeks before Easter and lasts several days until Ash Wednesday. In Freiburg, it mainly involves costume parties and parades with groups of people wearing oversized handmade masks and colorful patchwork costumes, often portraying witches or strange-looking creatures.

Alex wore a green dinosaur cape and looked adorable. Daniela dressed as the pantomime character Pierrot, wearing a white costume with black buttons down the front, complete with white face makeup that I put on her. She also had a cap that wouldn't stay on her head, because she had no hair to pin it to.

Joseph dressed up as a black cat and wore a long black wig. I painted his face for the occasion. I often thought Joseph missed his calling in life. He loved dressing up in wigs or as a woman for Halloween or Fasching. He enjoyed singing and being the center of attention—he could have been the first straight drag queen in Freiburg. The only problem was, he didn't make a pretty woman. He looked more like Tootsie or Mrs. Doubtfire.

I painted my face white and wore black tails borrowed from Joseph's concert clothing.

When we stayed in the house, the kids often played together. We had a swing that we could hang in the doorway to the children's bedroom. It was made of wood and had moveable bars on all sides so that Alex wouldn't fall out when he sat in it. After I put Alex in the swing, Daniela pulled herself up to stand on the back of the wooden seat. She held onto the ropes and swung her brother back and forth through the door frame. Alex loved it.

You would think I could have relaxed and appreciated this time together as a family. Yet a constant, nagging feeling of insecurity about Daniela's health prevented me from truly enjoying those moments to the fullest.

Europa Park Again

At the end of April 1994, I took Daniela to Europa Park. We rode the train through the park, and Daniela loved going down the slides and climbing the ladders and ropes in the huge playground called Wikiland. She would shout, "*Halloooo!*" into the tunnel slide and listen for the echo before sliding down. She also spent some time in the bouncy castle and loved diving into the pool of plastic balls. Her fine blond hair stuck out on all sides from static electricity, which actually looked kind of cute.

Daniela did *not* like the bumper cars. She took after me. I only wanted to drive around and not be bumped. She enjoyed the thrill of the children's roller coasters the most.

One week later, there was another excursion to Europa Park with nurses, parents, and children from the cancer ward who were well enough to go. It rained part of the time, but we still enjoyed the indoor rides and the ice skating and vaudeville shows.

In May 1994, several families from Daniela's kindergarten traveled to Falkau in the High Black Forest. At 1,277 meters, Falkau is the highest village in Germany. Joseph, Alex, Daniela, and I stayed for two days and spent the night in a cabin. One of the fathers even brought a guitar, and we sang songs around the campfire in the evening and baked *Stockbrot*—bread on a stick. I guessed that was the German equivalent to roasting marshmallows. We twisted some bread dough around the end of a whittled stick and held it over the open fire until it was baked—or burned, as was often the case.

Daniela danced to the guitar music. She was so musical, either singing, dancing, or both. I caught her on video at home holding a badminton racket like a guitar and pretending to be a country singer. Alex sat next to her on the couch, copying Daniela's movements in the air and using nonsense syllables. Daniela often encouraged Alex to sing and dance along. It was sweet.

The Story of the Blue Mittens

We made friends with a young Mormon family from Utah. The father had been transferred to work for an American company near Freiburg for a couple of years and brought his family with him. Their two kids were close to Daniela's and Alex's age.

In the fall of 1994, both of our families took a trip to *Mundenhof,* a small zoo in Freiburg. This was Daniela and Alex's first visit to a zoo.

Daniela wore her favorite bright blue mittens with a matching scarf and knitted cap. The mittens featured a crocheted mama bear on the right and a crocheted papa bear on the left. The scarf had a bear on each end, and the cap displayed them both on the front.

We pushed the children around in strollers and looked at all the animals. When we reached the monkeys, Joseph lifted Daniela out of her stroller and held her up close to the cage so she could see better.

As Daniela stretched her right hand toward the cage, a monkey lunged forward, reached through the bars, and snatched her mitten right off her hand. The other monkeys immediately joined in, pulling at the mitten until it began to unravel. It only took a few seconds for it to be destroyed.

Daniela burst into tears, devastated by the loss of her mitten. Her distress set off our friends' daughter, who also began to cry.

We finally calmed them down, even though we couldn't retrieve the mitten. I kept the remaining blue mitten, because I thought it was so cute.

Picture of Alex and Daniela

One day, I took Alex and Daniela to a department store to have their picture taken. When I later picked up the photos, I went without the kids and unexpectedly ran into my sixty-year-old piano student on my way.

I was surprised to see him. With Freiburg's population well over 220,000, I rarely ran into anyone I knew in the Old Town.

"Hello, Frau Webb. What are you doing here?" he asked.

"I just picked up some pictures of my kids," I said proudly. Without thinking, I pulled out the large photo of the two of them and showed it to him.

Daniela's head was completely bald.

"Oh!" he exclaimed, backing away from the picture.

I had never told him about Daniela's illness, and since I taught him in his home, he hadn't seen her since she lost her hair.

"Um, yeah, Daniela has cancer and has been going through chemotherapy," I stuttered. "But she's better now," I added hastily.

I felt awful for embarrassing him like that. Barely saying goodbye, I rushed out, leaving him standing there, speechless, with his mouth open.

Live Mannequin

During that same summer, Daniela and I were in a large department store in the children's clothing section. Child-sized mannequins were displayed throughout the store, modeling the newest styles. Daniela, who was wearing a summer hat to cover her bald head, stepped onto one of the small platforms and stood beside a child mannequin. Without any prompting from me, she raised her arms into a pose and froze, remaining absolutely still—even her eyes didn't move.

I stepped back, watching with amusement. It was fun to see shoppers pass by, then do a double take when they realized that one of the mannequins was actually a real child.

Cheap Barbie Doll

One afternoon, we took the kids to the Black Forest for a ride on the *Sommerrodelbahn*, an outdoor summer toboggan run. Joseph and Alex rode together on a double toboggan, while Daniela and I shared another.

The toboggans had a brake handle. Pushing it forward loosened the brake, allowing gravity to pull you faster down the mountain. Pulling it back slowed you down, which was best to do before curves to avoid flying off the track.

Even the chairlift ride up the mountainside felt like a treat, offering views of mountain goats, deer, and other animals enclosed in the park below. We rode the toboggans a couple of times, gaining confidence with each run and daring to go faster each time.

On our way back to Freiburg, we stopped at a typical Black Forest souvenir shop. Daniela saw Jasmine and Aladdin dolls from the Disney movie. She wanted Jasmine. The doll was overpriced and poorly made, far inferior to a real Barbie doll.

I didn't want to spend that much on such a cheap doll, so I told Daniela that she couldn't have it. She pitched a fit, crying all the way to the car. I stood firm, even though part of me wanted to buy her the doll—not just to end the conflict, but because I longed to spoil my little girl, who had already endured so much.

But we're not supposed to spoil our children—right?

She fussed and sobbed, but I felt the pressures of parenthood and didn't give in. It was horrible. The conflict pretty much ruined our outing.

Chapter 11

In Remission

Summer Vacation in Ibiza

Since Daniela was doing well during the summer of 1994, Joseph and I booked a two-week all-inclusive trip to Ibiza. It was our first trip to this Spanish island. We stayed at a hotel with a swimming pool located next to the Mediterranean Sea. Prior to the trip, I complained about the cost, but Joseph insisted that we go, which went against my financial principles. I was always one to save money for something I wanted and not to charge my credit card to the max, so I didn't feel good about knowing that we had overdrawn our account for the trip. (In Germany, you're allowed to overdraw up to a designated amount.) We would be paying interest until we could balance the account again.

The hotel rooms were arranged in a U-shape with two swimming pools in between and access to the ocean. The kids enjoyed swimming in the chlorinated pool more than in the salty ocean water. However, when we did go to the beach, both Alex and Daniela had a blast burying their dad in the sand until only his head was peeping out. We also went to a water park called *Aguamar* and enjoyed the nightly entertainment at the hotel.

On the first night, Joseph and I decided to attend one of the outdoor resort shows after putting the kids to bed. About thirty minutes into the show, an announcement was made that two children were awake and standing on their balcony. Joseph and I exchanged glances, instinctively knowing that those kids must be ours. There was no way they were going to stay asleep with all the music blaring, so Joseph went back to the room and brought them to the show.

I had been randomly chosen to join an improvised sketch, so the kids had a blast watching their mom on stage pantomiming a cavewoman, grunting and moving around hunched over like a Neanderthal. It was great fun getting a large, appreciative audience to laugh.

We enjoyed that vacation to the fullest as a family, except for one thing: the rooms were not provided with fresh water. We had to brush our teeth and shower with saltwater. The advertisement had said nothing about the water in the rooms being salty. Should we have known that?

Regular Checkups

On October 7, 1994, Joseph and I were called into a meeting with Dr. Zimmermann.

"We're working with statistics and numbers from yesterday on patients from today," she said, "but we believe that Daniela is in full remission from her neuroblastoma."

They never say cancer is cured. Instead, you are "in remission" — a safe way for the doctors to say that you don't have any signs or symptoms of cancer at the moment. They never commit to saying that the cancer is totally gone, because it could still be lurking somewhere, like a bear in winter. One day, it might awaken—showing its ugly teeth and consuming healthy cells again.

"However," she began.

All hope of Daniela's remission was destroyed with that one word, "however."

"Daniela has suffered damage to her bone marrow from the chemotherapy. This will likely get better, but it may take six months to a year." She further explained that Daniela would continue to receive palliative therapy and transfusions as necessary to manage symptoms until her bone marrow recovered.

Even though she was in remission, the hospital visits continued. Our plan for follow-up care looked like this:

- **First year:** A checkup every six weeks, with a blood sample taken at every other appointment.

- **Every three months:** An ultrasound of her abdomen, a CT scan, an MRI, a chest x-ray, and a urine sample.

- **No live vaccinations** for at least six months.

Would these trips to the hospital ever end?

Chapter 12

More Illness in the Family

When things were going smoothly with Daniela, and after the doctors declared her in remission, Alex started limping and showing signs of pain. At two and a half years of age, he was too young to tell us where it hurt, so a radiologist performed a CT scan of his knees and hips. They thought he might have some kind of hip dysplasia, but the CT results came back normal.

Alex's symptoms were similar to those that Daniela had at the beginning, so the doctors felt they needed to rule out neuroblastoma. Fear grew inside me like a vine choking a bush. I kept thinking about Martin's family with five children, two of whom had had leukemia, and dreaded the possibility that Alex might have the same thing as Daniela.

By then, more than two years after Daniela's diagnosis, a urine test had been initiated to screen for neuroblastoma. In our first attempt to gather some urine from Alex for the screening, a nurse taped a urine bag onto him, and we covered it with a diaper.

Well, I swear Alex went all day without peeing. He must have sensed something was off and held it in. Finally, we gave up. Sure enough, as soon as we removed the bag, Alex soaked his diaper. It took several days, but we finally got a urine sample. When Alex's test for neuroblastoma came back negative, our relief was palpable.

Still, we didn't know what was wrong with him and we wouldn't know for another eight weeks. Those eight weeks of uncertainty felt like a volcano about to erupt.

Toward the end of that time, Alex started holding the back of his hand to his lower back and saying, *"Au-wa!"*

I told the doctor that it looked like Alex's pain was radiating from his back. The radiologist ordered another MRI, this time including his lower back. The scan revealed spondylodiscitis—a rare infection of the disc, with possible secondary infection of the vertebrae. The doctor told us this condition rarely happened in children under thirteen. In fact, the incidence of spondylodiscitis was just seven per million.

Instead of being able to enjoy Daniela's time in remission, we were confronted with Alex's illness. The unrelenting stress felt unbearable.

Because Alex's condition had gone untreated for some time, the infection had spread to the surrounding lumbar vertebrae—L4 and L5—which were eroded on the sides adjacent to the infected disc.

The treatment required keeping Alex immobile and administering IV antibiotics. He was fitted with a half-body plaster cast, extending from his shoulders to the back of his thighs. Velcro fastenings held him on his back and prevented movement. He remained in the cast for almost two weeks at the Children's Hospital—though in a different ward than his sister had been.

A follow-up exam showed that the infection was gone, and the disc was hardly visible. The doctor explained that the two vertebrae had fused together, making him less flexible in that part of his back, but he shouldn't have any major trouble with it.

Given our kids' uncanny tendency to develop rare diseases, I found humor even in our darkest hours. I would tell people, "With the odds in our family, I should play the lottery—I would probably have a decent shot at winning." But I never actually did. I viewed the lottery as a waste of money.

A Grandmother's Wisdom

I had always been close to my grandmother, Elizabeth, on my father's side of the family. We called her Grandmother Lizzy, or Grandma Lizzy for short.

When I called to update her on Daniela's remission and Alex's health issues, I said, "Why does this have to happen to me?"

"It builds character," she said.

"Well, I could do without that much character," I joked.

But she was right. Someone once compared life to a lump of coal—our experiences, both good and bad, have the power to shape us into diamonds, depending on how we handle them. I often looked for the lighter side, made jokes, and found ways to make people laugh—even when laughter may not seem appropriate—because humor can offer relief.

Friends sometimes claimed I was "always in a good mood." If only they knew. I worked hard not to let my sadness or depression show, appearing strong on the outside—even when I felt like crying on the inside.

When Grandma Lizzy turned eighty-three and was sick with cancer of the bladder, I promised her, "If you're still alive after Christmas, I'll come visit you with Daniela."

I kept that promise.

Letter to Family (Tues., Dec. 19, 1994)

Alex came home from the hospital on Friday evening. We were all exhausted Saturday, and yesterday we were stressed with Daniela's birthday party. We had invited six children (three from church and three from Daniela's kindergarten). It was fun for her, but definitely stressful for us. Christmas will be spent quietly with the four of us. We may join some friends of ours on Christmas Eve. Joseph has to play Tannhäuser (a four-hour-long opera) on the afternoon of the 25th, so we'll probably cook a turkey on the 26th, which is also a holiday here in Germany.

Alex is walking again, but he's walking funny. I thought he was pain-free until today when he said "au-wa" while sitting in his booster chair. When I asked him where his "au-wa" was, he said "da unten, im Popo" (down in my butt). He's taking antibiotics at home for the next two weeks. On Friday, we'll see the doctor, so I can ask her about his walking. They had originally said he would need physical therapy, but when he was released from the hospital, they didn't prescribe it. The health reform here has caused doctors to make lots of cuts in prescribing things like physical therapy, 80%–90% of which is paid for by the health insurance.

Five Years Old

On Daniela's fifth birthday, she unwrapped one of her presents—a video. She held it out to us, and we read the title for her: *Bambi*. Due to her illnesses and hospitalizations, she had only been able to attend kindergarten sporadically and couldn't read. Although children in Germany typically didn't learn to read in kindergarten, I often read to her in English. She was learning to speak both German and English and could write her first name in capital letters, though she often wrote the "E" backwards.

By then, her hair had grown into a cute pixie cut. She had never had a haircut during those five years. Her hair had started falling out from chemotherapy by her third birthday, and continued treatment stunted its growth. One of her friends gave her a headband as a present, though I think she wore it only on her birthday.

While Daniela sat around the table with her six friends, everyone dug into my carrot cake—except for Daniela. I made my carrot cake with fresh-ground whole wheat and vegetable oil, which made it very moist and tasty. I topped it with a luscious icing made from butter, powdered sugar, cream cheese, and vanilla. So, I couldn't understand why Daniela didn't want any.

"Don't you want some cake, Daniela?"

She shook her head.

"More for us, then!" I said, hiding my disappointment.

Daniela had a wonderful birthday at home, surrounded by friends and family. We all had a good time. One of my family members had been thoughtful enough to send a gift to Alex so he wouldn't feel left out while Daniela opened her presents.

He got a plastic car, about the size of a softball, and played with it for a few minutes.

"*Auto 'put*," Alex said.

"Oh no," I exclaimed. "The car is kaputt?"

"Yeah."

Well, it was the thought that counted, right?

Another family member had sent Daniela "taps" as a gift: two big pink plastic bows that strapped around her ankles and clicked with every step. Daniela put on her new camisole and tights, slipped into black dress shoes, and fastened the taps, then danced around the apartment to the music Joseph had turned on. She climbed onto the pine coffee table and continued to dance, moving and grooving to South American rhythms. I didn't care about the coffee table. It was a wonderful sight to behold our healthy, energetic five-year-old daughter so full of life.

Chapter 13

Trip to the US

In December 1994, I booked a flight to Atlanta to take Daniela to visit my family in Georgia and Florida, including Grandma Lizzy, who was still alive.

At one of Daniela's regular checkups, her white blood cell (WBC) count had increased to around 30,000. (The normal level ranges from 4,500 to 10,000 per microliter.) Her WBCs continued to rise, causing flaky stools or diarrhea. One week before the flight, Daniela came down with a fever. Dr. Zimmermann told me she didn't think it would be wise to fly with Daniela to the U.S. or take her on a long trip.

I still had the assurance that my brother-in-law was a pediatrician—even though he primarily worked in research—so I called him that night.

"How's Daniela doing?" he asked.

"Not too good. Her white blood cells are really high."

"How high?"

"30,000."

"30,000! That can't be right. There must be some mistake."

I assured him that it was correct, but he still couldn't believe it.

Wanting to keep my promise and see Grandma Lizzy one last time, I took the risk, packed our bags, and headed to the Frankfurt Airport with Daniela.

Railway Mission

In Germany, if you have a physical or mental disability—or cancer—you can apply for a disability ID card, which the hospital automatically did for all of their young cancer patients. With Daniela's disability ID, we were able to enlist the help of the *Bahnhofsmission* (Railway Mission), a social services organization that helps people navigate the train station.

In order to reach the Frankfurt Airport, we had to take a tram and two trains, switching trains in Mannheim. I contacted the Railway Mission ahead of time, letting them know which rail car we were on. An older woman from the Railway Mission met us on the platform in Mannheim. While I pushed Daniela in a stroller, she helped us with our luggage.

After taking one look at Daniela, the woman said, "She doesn't look disabled."

Her comment sounded more curious than offensive—I suppose most of the people she helps have a visible disability.

In a hushed tone, I told her that Daniela had cancer.

She took another look at Daniela, this time with pity in her expression.

Wanting to ease that pity, I assured her that Daniela was currently in remission. Although, with Daniela's symptoms, I wasn't too sure anymore.

On the Plane

Daniela still had a fever and loose stools. When we began our trip, she had some belly pain and even threw up once on the train. I had no idea how I was going to get us through the ten-hour flight.

Optimistic and excited to see family, Daniela told me, "*Im Flugzeug werde ich krank sein, aber in Amerika werde ich nicht krank sein.*" ("On the plane, I'll be sick, but in America, I won't be sick.")

The travel agency had supposedly reserved our seats, but the only two adjacent ones left were in the smoking section, which has since been eliminated from all international flights. One person in front of us and a couple to our right smoked, but the ventilation was so good that it was tolerable. We sat in the last row, and after settling in, I checked to see where the closest toilet was. Daniela no longer wore diapers, so with her soft stools, she might need to go to the restroom frequently. We were fortunate to be at the back of the plane, because the toilets were right behind us.

The turbulence made us both feel queasy, so I gave Daniela half of a pill for motion sickness. I hoped the active ingredient, dimenhydrinate, would help her rest, as it always made me feel drowsy.

I gave her a pillow and covered her with a blanket. She leaned against the airplane window and soon fell asleep. She slept on and off for most of the flight and had no diarrhea. It was amazing—nothing short of a miracle!

Visiting Family in Georgia

Before landing in Atlanta, Daniela said she wanted to go home and be with Alex. Alex was still recovering from his pain, so I left him at home with Joseph in order to have time to focus on Daniela and my family.

Once we were on the ground and with loving family members who paid attention to her, Daniela no longer felt homesick. She smiled when my older sister, Olivia, and one of Lynn's sons greeted her at the airport, but she barely spoke a word to anyone and acted unusually shy.

We all spent the night at Olivia's house. Aside from Lynn's sons, Lynn was there, too, so it was a real treat for me. Lynn gave us two Dr. Seuss videos (including *One Fish, Two Fish, Red Fish, Blue Fish*) that my maternal grandmother, Nana, had given to Lynn's sons the previous year, when they were already fourteen and twelve years old—long after they had outgrown Dr. Seuss videos! My kids were still young enough to appreciate them.

It was all very overwhelming for Daniela. By 6:30 p.m., which was 12:30 a.m. in Germany, she said she was tired and wanted to go to bed. I put her to bed, and my nephew even read a book to her. Meanwhile, Olivia picked up some chicken and biscuits, which we ate with some homemade mashed potatoes and green bean casserole. Given Daniela's upset stomach, she wouldn't have eaten anyway, so it was just as well that she slept.

The next day we visited Nana in Gainesville, Georgia. It was a brief visit—long enough for her to see her great-granddaughter—before we headed to my parents' home in Blairsville.

Daniela had a great time visiting her grandparents. They were into flying kites and stunt kites back then and even sewed their own. They drove us out to an open field to fly their kites. Daniela was thrilled to see the stunt kite soaring through the air and making acrobatic movements.

That night, my mom cooked a delicious meal, and my dad told us stories from his past. He was a great storyteller. Sometimes he would make things up, such as saying that the tines of a fork were named after a man named Robert Tine. We were impressed until we saw him suppressing a grin, and then we knew he had made it up. We all laughed at our gullibility.

After being doted on by my parents, it was time for Daniela to say goodbye. We flew to Tampa to visit Grandma Lizzy.

My grandmother looked very frail—her face was bony, and she had dark rings under her eyes. I witnessed several times how she would walk from one room to the next and have to stop to catch her breath. She used her oxygen frequently.

Daniela bonded with her great-grandmother when Grandma Lizzy offered to read one of her books to her. It didn't matter that I had read the book to her countless times—she snuggled up close to her great-grandmother and listened attentively.

Grandma Lizzy and I both cried as we said goodbye. Deep down, I knew it would be the last time I would see her.

Chapter 14

Disney World

After we left my grandmother's, I took Daniela to Disney World in Orlando. At the Magic Kingdom, Daniela and I rode the monorail and train, climbed the Swiss Family Treehouse, and explored Tom Sawyer's Island. Daniela was too small to go on Splash Mountain or the roller coasters, but we visited other attractions such as Peter Pan's Flight, Pirates of the Caribbean, the Country Bear Jamboree, and It's a Small World. Daniela loved all the dolls from around the world—and I hummed that song for the rest of the day, much to my dismay.

She especially enjoyed a live presentation of *The Lion King* with the large puppets, and we both loved the stage presentation of *Beauty and the Beast*. A woman dressed as Belle sang live, accompanied by all the life-sized characters from the castle. The story was condensed into about twenty-five minutes, and the music from the Disney musical was great as always.

When we went to MGM Studios (now called Disney's Hollywood Studios), we rode *Star Tours*, a flight simulator that takes you on a journey through *Star Wars* scenes. You sit in a spaceship and look out through the front window, viewing flying scenes while the entire capsule you're in moves and jerks you about. You really feel like you're in the movie. I imagine Daniela thought we had actually traveled through space. She was in awe when we exited the ride and returned to the park.

However, one of the best attractions we experienced was the Tower of Terror. Based on an episode from *The Twilight Zone*, the ride is a haunted service elevator gone rogue that drops you from the 13th floor. It was the most thrilling attraction I have ever been on, and I highly recommend it.

We entered an old building with dated furniture covered with cobwebs and watched a *Twilight Zone* introduction, complete with a good impression of Rod Serling's voice to set the mood. Merely waiting in line made me feel nervous. We took a seat in the service elevator and rode up to the top floor. The elevator doors opened, and the elevator moved forward, out of the shaft and down the hall. I was impressed by that effect, since I had no idea how they made the elevator do that. When we reached the other side, we entered another shaft, and then the elevator dropped free-fall for several feet. It was a breathtaking experience, and I think I laughed hysterically, as I often do whenever I ride roller coasters.

Daniela screamed. It reminded me of when she watched Disney's *Alice in Wonderland*. Every time Alice fell into the rabbit hole, Daniela screamed—no matter how many times she had seen the video.

The elevator caught hold, of course, and we slowed to a stop instead of crashing to the bottom. It was fun and thrilling.

When we got off the ride, I turned on the video camera and interviewed Daniela.

"Did you like the Tower of Terror?"

Daniela stood there, covering her mouth with both hands, and nodded.

"Were you scared?"

She nodded slowly.

"Do you wanna do it again?"

This time, she nodded emphatically and smiled.

I was amazed that Daniela enjoyed all of these scary things. She was the perfect age for our trip.

The Parade

It was time for the daily parade. All the Disney characters we knew and loved were walking along Main Street, U.S.A.: Belle and the Beast, Mickey and Minnie Mouse, Snow White and the Seven Dwarfs, and even Alice and the White Rabbit—all in life-sized, realistic-looking costumes.

I wanted to get a better view and film some of the parade, but the people in front of me were taller, blocking my view. Daniela squeezed through the person in front of me to stand at the edge of the street to watch. I told her to stay right where she was while I climbed onto a nearby bench to film the parade.

A moment later, the parade was over. The crowd along the edge of the street began to disperse. When I returned to where I had left Daniela, she wasn't there!

I spun around, looking in all directions.

All of a sudden, the street was full of people.

Daniela was nowhere in sight.

I turned to the first person nearby, a middle-aged woman, and asked, "Did you see a little girl with curly blond hair and a red top?"

"No, I'm sorry," she said apologetically, as if it were her fault. "Maybe she went into that building over there."

She pointed to the entrance of a nearby attraction. I quickly checked it out, but Daniela wasn't there either.

I returned to where she had last stood. Taking a breath and closing my eyes, I told myself, *All right. Don't panic. If I were Daniela, where would I go?*

I instantly knew the answer.

I would join the parade!

I rushed down the street in the direction that the parade was headed.

As I approached the last characters in the parade, I spotted Daniela marching to the music behind them. I caught up with her, fell into step with the music, and grinned down at her.

"Wasn't that a great parade?"

Daniela looked up at me with a big smile on her face. "Mm hmm," she nodded.

I was so grateful that I found her before she started missing me that I didn't even think to scold her. She was doing what any healthy child would do— marching in a parade!

Besides, *I had lost her,* and it was my fault.

After following the parade for a short while, Daniela looked up at me and said, "Can we go back to the Terrible Tower?"

"Of course we can."

So, the last thing we did before leaving the park was to ride the Tower of Terror again.

Daniela screamed the second time around, too. I felt less nervous since I knew what was coming, but that awful feeling of falling was still terrible—and thrilling!

Last Day in the US

During the entire two weeks, Daniela had no diarrhea and no fever. We experienced beautiful weather in Orlando—warm with clear skies. We were lucky, because it rained the day we drove back to the Tampa airport.

Our trip home went without delays. Daniela only slept for two hours, but the flight from Atlanta to Frankfurt was about one hour shorter because of the tailwinds.

Joseph picked us up from the train station.

When I was unloading Daniela from the car, I found small, crumbled pieces of glass on the car seat.

"What happened?" I asked.

"Fourteen cars were broken into in the parking garage, including ours."

"And you didn't think to tell me about it?"

"I didn't want to ruin your trip."

Whoever broke into our car left our radio and the child car seat but took my black bag and two plastic boxes from the trunk, which contained vitamin supplements from our network marketing business, as well as other small security products and tools—amounting to about $400.

Our insurance company wouldn't cover the business items because they claimed they should have been insured separately. From then on, we no longer stored the products in the car and left the back cover open so that potential thieves could see the trunk was empty.

Alex and Daniela especially enjoyed seeing each other again. They both hugged, and Alex followed Daniela around the apartment.

The next evening, I had to go to my choral rehearsal. Alex must have thought I was leaving for another two weeks because he cried and clung to me like he never had before. Joseph had gone to play a symphony concert, so the babysitter needed to comfort him.

We made another role switch. Joseph would be primarily responsible for the network marketing business, along with his orchestra job, while I was responsible for cooking, cleaning, getting the kids to school, and taking Daniela to her doctor appointments.

I noticed I became much more patient with the children since I had less stress and pressure. Joseph said we should have made the switch much sooner. He forgot that for months I had been saying he should handle the business, and I would make sure lunch was on the table. He hadn't been ready, I guess.

But life wasn't all roses. The very next day after we returned home to Freiburg, Daniela developed a fever and diarrhea.

Her prediction had come true: *I won't be sick in America.*

Back Home

Before Daniela and I had left for Atlanta, I was terrified and suspected her cancer might have returned. But rather than postponing our flight, I figured the two weeks wouldn't make much of a difference. I absolutely wanted my family and Daniela to see each other—afraid that if we didn't go then, we might not be able to go the following summer if she were sick again. I was glad we made the trip to see family and was grateful that I could share some memorable times with her at Disney World.

Two days after we returned home, with Daniela still experiencing loose stools, I took her to the doctor. We found out that her white blood cells had increased to 59,600, which was way too high. Her hemoglobin was low at 9.9, and she only had 27,000 platelets.

Because her blood count didn't make sense, the doctor suspected it might be a recurrence of her cancer and wanted to check her bone marrow. She didn't have a fever when I took her in to see him, but by bedtime, Daniela's temperature had risen to 102.2°F (39°C). The appointment for the bone marrow aspiration was set for two days later.

Another grueling wait.

After that doctor's appointment, I felt depressed and scared. I cried off and on throughout the day. Try as I might, I couldn't stop the negative thoughts. I remembered the doctors telling us that if her cancer should return—and she had about an 85–90% chance that it would—they wouldn't know what to do with her, because she had already gone through such intensive therapy during the first round.

Since Joseph and I rarely talked about our feelings regarding Daniela's health, I didn't know how he felt, but I sensed that he wasn't doing well either.

In two days, we would know more—at least whether the bone marrow was free of cancer cells or not.

Olivia wrote me letters and sent them by fax because we both owned one, and the letter arrived instantly.

She wrote that she was sorry to hear about the medical news but felt that everything was going to be fine. She encouraged me to remind Daniela that she had to get well so she could go to Georgia and do fun things every year. Then, when she became a mom, she could do fun things with her kids.

That was sweet of my sister to focus on Daniela being cured and becoming a mom herself. I wanted to believe Olivia. I always imagined my daughter growing up and having kids of her own.

But when the doctors rattled off that list of chemo side effects, one thing stuck with me after the fuzziness cleared: children—girls in particular—who undergo chemotherapy at a young age can experience infertility as a late effect, one that may not show up until years later.

Girls are born with all the egg cells they'll ever have. At puberty, one matures each month until menopause. But some chemotherapy drugs can destroy those immature egg cells—

quietly, irreversibly—making it impossible for a girl who survives cancer to conceive as an adult.

It saddened me deeply to think that Daniela might never be able to have a child of her own.

95

Chapter 15

A Second Malignancy

I took Daniela into the examination room. This time, when the doctor took a sample of her bone marrow, he didn't bother to sedate her. I don't know why. Not enough time? Not enough staff? Or maybe they thought she could handle it.

Daniela had to lie on her stomach while the doctor used an instrument that resembled a hand-held corkscrew with a straight needle.

Daniela screamed in pain as the large needle was screwed into her pelvis bone with rotating motions. I stroked her head, trying to comfort her, but her anguish continued.

"Shh. It'll be alright," I whispered, though I felt awful. As a mother, I should have been able to protect her from this pain. Instead, I had to suffer with her, feeling her cries deep in my tensed muscles.

When the results came back, our worst fears were confirmed. We learned that Daniela's bone marrow had been so damaged by chemotherapy that she had developed Chronic Myelomonocytic Leukemia (CMML), also referred to as Juvenile Myelomonocytic Leukemia in the U.S. This is a type of chronic blood cancer in which a person's bone marrow produces too many white blood cells (monocytes), which explains the alarming increase in Daniela's blood count.

Joseph had been right. Daniela had received too much chemotherapy.

Dr. Zimmerman told us that the only possible cure for CMML was a bone marrow transplant (also called allogeneic or hematopoietic stem cell transplant). This involves injecting healthy stem cells to replace diseased bone marrow. However, the malfunctioning bone marrow first has to be destroyed with new rounds of chemotherapy.

When will this nightmare end?

Letter to Family (Wed., Feb. 8, 1995)

Dear Mommy and Daddy,

Yesterday, Daniela had to receive some platelets—her third transfusion in 2-1/2 weeks. The doctors predicted she would need transfusions every couple of days, so she's doing better than they expected.

We're still awaiting the results of Alex and Daniela's bone marrow typing to see if they match. If she needs a bone marrow transplant, it will involve a lot less risk if the donor is a brother or sister. Otherwise, it could take two to four months (or more) to find a donor, and the match wouldn't be as good as with a sibling.

Daniela complains of being tired (her hemoglobin is hovering around 8.0), but otherwise, she seems fine—except for the dark bruises she gets. We went swimming on Saturday, and as Daniela was undressing, I thought someone is going to think she's a battered child!

Alex occasionally walks stiffly and complains of pain in his back, so I think he needs to be checked. But with all the time I spend with Daniela at the doctor's, I haven't gotten around to making an appointment for Alex.

I'm so sick of waiting around for doctors. We have to go in almost every day (an average of five days a week) to have Daniela's blood checked. Ideally, I'd like to take her in for a finger prick before kindergarten and then call later to find out the results, since it takes at least 45 minutes for the results to come back. The platelets have to be counted by hand.

Joseph went home this week to see his family in Bavaria and wanted to take Daniela, but her platelets were so low that we thought it best for her to stay here. He would have to spend his days in Bavaria with Daniela in a clinic, which isn't a vacation for him.

Alex is making messes again. I don't know if he's acting his age, or if he's trying to get attention—perhaps a bit of both.

Alex now says his name. It comes out sounding like "Palace," which always makes me laugh. He also says "fuvfoo" for "I love you." In fact, all the initial consonants are wrong, but the vowel sounds are right. It took me a while to figure out that when Alex said, "pooping bum," he meant "chewing gum." I'm wondering if he has a speech defect.

I can only say thank God we live in Germany, where there is social medicine, and all costs for caring for sick children are covered. I suppose no insurance company would cover Daniela if we wanted to move to the U.S., since she has a pre-existing condition. It's saddening to think I may have to live in Germany until Daniela has been in remission for at least five years. Maybe the U.S. will move to social medicine before then. (Hasn't there been some talk about it?)

All my love,
Tracey

Info on HLA Compatibility

Human leukocyte antigen (HLA) typing is used to find a match for a bone marrow donor. Unlike blood, which has three factors, the HLA has several factors, and a minimum of six need to match for the transplant to be successful and without complications.

A child receives half of their HLA markers from each parent, which means a parent can never be a full match for their child. A sibling, however, has a 25% chance of being a match. When I learned that Daniela's CMML could only be cured with a bone marrow transplant, I felt certain that Alex would be her donor. But Dr. Zimmermann informed us that Alex's HLA didn't have enough matches.

I was crushed. I had clung to the belief that he would fit. It felt like the one thing we could count on.

This meant that we had to wait for the bone marrow database to come up with a better match. A simple swab of the cheek is used to determine if someone was a close bone marrow match. If a potential donor has the basic matches, further testing is done to determine compatibility, either through blood tests or more cheek swabs.

My patience was being tested once again.

Death in the Family

Life delivered yet another blow. While we were waiting to hear about a possible bone marrow donor, Daddy called me to let me know that Grandmother Lizzy passed away on February 16, 1995. He didn't inform me until the evening before the funeral, leaving me no chance to catch a flight from Germany and arrive in time for the service.

"You've got enough on your plate," he said. "You don't need to fly over here to be at the funeral."

He was right, of course. Nevertheless, I was saddened that it wouldn't be possible for me to attend my favorite grandmother's funeral.

The next day, while the service was being held in Tampa, Florida, I sat at my piano and played music for my grandmother. She had wanted me to play at her funeral, so I played a solo concert for her from home. I felt far away from everyone, from everything—but playing for her helped bridge that distance.

Journal Entry (Sun., Feb. 26, 1995)

We found out on Friday (two days ago) that Alex is <u>not</u> HLA identical to Daniela, which means he cannot be a bone marrow donor for her. There are two mismatches, which would make the transplant a very high risk—higher than using a registry donor who is HLA identical.

Now they have to find a donor, which can take a minimum of two months, but possibly longer. We hope that Daniela's condition doesn't worsen to the point that it would be too late to perform a transplant.

I was so disappointed and couldn't understand how this could be, especially since I had been visualizing for Alex to match. Joseph has hopes that Daniela will miraculously get well without the need for a transplant. Since we can't move forward with the transplant right now, it gives us more time for a miracle to occur. That's definitely what it would take.

Do I believe in miracles? I keep asking myself that question. Some days, the answer is yes. Other days, I don't know what I believe anymore. All I know is that we can't decide anything at the moment. It's all in God's hands.

Daniela's condition has worsened some. She had another transfusion of platelets yesterday, her fifth in five weeks, meaning she no longer has two weeks but one week between transfusions.

Daniela has developed an abscess on her butt, and the doctors want to give her antibiotics (Bactrim), but Joseph is against it, because it would ruin all we've been trying to do to strengthen her immune system and cleanse her bowels with homeopathic medicine. If it doesn't get better within a few days—and so far it seems to be getting worse—we'll have to give her antibiotics anyway, with much trepidation.

This week we sold our Honda Aerodeck to a car dealer and bought a five-year-old Honda Accord, so we've reduced our monthly car payments by more than two-thirds, and we're paying the bank instead of a leasing company. We're trying to find other ways to cut our costs since I can't work, now that I'm at the hospital with Daniela four or five times a week.

Joseph is taking over the network marketing business, and he seems to be enjoying it, although he overworks himself. We'll see what kind of fruits it will bring. I've been suggesting for some time that we switch roles. I help him with the paperwork and computer work, and he does the contacting and appointments. He seems happier now that he's not doing so much housework and has work that helps him grow.

What about me? Well, women tend to be stronger than men emotionally. Joseph can't handle the hospital visits anymore. He says they really depress him. They depress me too, but I get over it more quickly, I guess.

Yesterday, Aaron's mother told me that he has a recurrence of his neuroblastoma, this time in his brain. There's nothing the doctors can do for him except pump him full of morphine and cortisone. His face has swollen so much that you can barely recognize him. Four weeks ago, the doctors gave him hours or days to live. He got sick around the same time as Daniela and is three months shy of his fourth birthday.

Those are the kind of things we experience, but we don't experience them as outsiders like doctors and nurses, but as parents who are afraid of losing their child. That makes visualizing for me even more difficult.

Joseph saw Daniela as a 20-year-old with blond, wavy hair. She was very active. I heard him tell his horn teacher—who is retiring and will be spending his time healing people—that he thinks she'll make it. But on the other hand, he also said it feels as if she has given up.

When we tell Daniela to make more platelets or better blood, she now says that she can't do it by herself. I don't know how to help her.

Basel Zoo

In March 1995 we went on a family outing to the zoo in Basel, Switzerland. The zoo has a large aquarium and all the animals you could think of, including kangaroos. Or were they wallabies? It's hard to remember exactly.

We pushed Alex around in a stroller. By then, his back had recovered, but he was still too young to do all that walking through the zoo.

Daniela, on the other hand, had to walk. But after a while she suddenly stopped.

"I can't walk anymore. I'm tired."

She sounded so pitiful. We had to cut our trip short and take her home.

For those couple of hours, Daniela's cancer seemed far away—until we were whisked back to reality.

Still, we held on to that fleeting sense of normalcy. Shortly afterward, during Easter vacation, we visited Daniela's aunt and cousin in Bavaria. Daniela was in high spirits. She watched *Snow White and the Seven Dwarfs* on video, and we turned it into a game: she would act out a dwarf, and I had to guess which one.

She folded her arms and put a frown on her face.

"You must be Grumpy," I laughed. "What does Sneezy do?"

Daniela faked a sneeze.

"What does Dopey look like?"

Daniela pulled the sleeves of her sweatshirt down past her hands, just like his oversized shirt.

I smiled at how cute and perceptive she was. Even in the middle of everything, Daniela still knew how to play. Still knew how to bring joy.

Chapter 16

Family Rehab at Katharinenhöhe

On March 23, 1995, I found out on short notice that a family rehab (called a "Kur" in German) had been approved. Six days later, Daniela, Alex, and I went to a rehab center called *Katharinenhöhe* in Schönwald, in the Black Forest—only about a one-hour drive from Freiburg. Joseph drove us there but didn't stay with us.

Typically, children go to rehab following their treatment, but we were an exception and were allowed to go before treatment began. We spent four weeks at *Katharinenhöhe*, and all expenses were covered by health insurance. This family-oriented rehab center consists of several buildings, including a cafeteria, numerous clinic and therapy rooms, and a swimming pool. It offers thirty-five family apartments with a total of 120 beds, surrounded by forest and offering breathtaking mountain views. The center provides a peaceful retreat for families to recover after the harrowing experience of treating their child's serious illness.

Journal Entry (Thurs., Mar. 30, 1995)

Daniela is playing in the "Räuberhöhle" or "Lion's Den," her new kindergarten, while Alex and Joseph play in the snow. This gives me a few minutes to write my first impressions of Katharinenhöhe, a rehabilitation center for families with children who have cancer.

We arrived last evening to a beautiful winter wonderland. The snow in Freiburg melted, but up here at 1,000 meters (3,280 feet), it's piled high. We have a very nice two-room apartment with a toilet, shower, dining table and four chairs, a kitchenette with a tiny refrigerator, a stove with two burners, and a cabinet full of dishes. It's much nicer than the room we had in Bad Oexen, where we had no possibility of heating up food, cooling drinks, or even sitting at a table to eat or play.

The only thing we don't have in our room is an intercom system, which the babysitters or parents in Bad Oexen could use in the evenings when the children were asleep.

Everyone has been extremely helpful these first two days. The dining room operates like a restaurant, and there is a bar where we can buy ice cream and drinks until 10:30 p.m.

After dinner last night, we all went swimming. The kids didn't get to bed until almost 10:00 p.m.

This morning, we had a doctor's appointment at the rehab center. Daniela, Alex and I were all checked up, and we will receive a schedule of appropriate therapies and activities.

Our tour of the buildings was interrupted by an appointment with the psychologist. Joseph and I had a nice talk with her, informing her of our challenges related to Daniela. Alex was with us and started to get impatient until Daniela showed up. When Daniela started picking on Alex and things got loud, Joseph halted our conversation, saying that he couldn't have a session with all the noise and complaining that this had been the case for years. He also claimed that since he won't be here, he won't be having any sessions with the psychologist.

Joseph drove us to Katharinenhöhe, but he isn't joining us for rehab.

After our nice lunch of chicken, salad, French fries, and chocolate pudding, we went outside to play in the snow for an hour and a half. We used two sleds that a friend had lent us, and it was great fun for the whole family.

Rehab Activities

At rehab, Daniela went to kindergarten and Alex to nursery school in the mornings and occasionally in the afternoons. During that time, I had physical therapy (for my neck and back), massages, water aerobics (together with fifteen other parents), relaxation sessions in a group, four private sessions with the psychologist, and three group discussions with other parents and the psychologist I had for individual sessions. Compared to Daniela, I had so many more appointments. When I received our schedule, I exclaimed, "Who's the patient?"

It was great to be able to finally take some time for *myself* for a change. I attended some arts and crafts courses and made a flowerpot and a little round jar with a lid in pottery class. I also tried silk painting for the first time in my life. I had always wanted to know how it's done. I painted a scarf with swirls of red, green, and yellow, allowing the colors to bleed into each other. This was intentional wording, as I made yellow splotches to represent Daniela's thrombocytes, which she needed more of to help clot her blood.

I also painted a tie with swirly colors of blue. It would have been beautiful, except that some bleached spots appeared on the large part of the tie that showed, and there was no way to get rid of them or cover them up. I thought about cutting it off and making it into a smaller tie for Alex to wear to church, but I never got around to it.

Joseph visited us for Easter and one other time. During our rehab, he went on a trip with his orchestra to Granada, Spain. Then he flew from there to Amsterdam for the first European convention of the network marketing company we were part of. I would have liked to have gone, too, but I was in Schönwald with the kids.

Even if I had been at home and able to go, I wouldn't have known anyone who could take care of the kids for five days. I didn't want to leave them with a babysitter for that long, especially since Daniela needed blood transfusions during that time.

Aristocats

I took a few video cassettes with us to *Katharinenhöhe* and spread the word that we would be watching Walt Disney's *Aristocats* at 3 o'clock. Several children came to the TV room to watch it with us.

When we got to Alex and Daniela's favorite part—the scene where the street cats play music and sing "Everybody, everybody, everybody wants to be a cat!"—they did exactly what they always did at home. They jumped up and sang along at the top of their lungs, stomping their feet and clapping their hands.

The other children gave them strange looks, as if they were crazy, which made me laugh even more. One of the kids yelled, "Quiet! I can't hear!" but Daniela and Alex didn't stop until the song was over.

Day 4 of Rehab

On the fourth night into our rehab, Daniela had a small accident. She was walking across some chairs when she lost her balance and fell, trapping her left leg between two of them. A thick blue bruise with red dots formed on her thigh. It looked awful.

Meanwhile, the wound from the abscess on her butt was taking a long time to heal.

That night, I was disturbed about something Alex did.

We had eaten some ice cream before heading back to our room. As we walked down the hallway, Daniela opened a door and stepped through. Alex, walking to my left in the wide corridor, smacked straight into the wall next to the door. He bumped his forehead, leaving a chocolate smudge from the ice cream on his mouth.

"Alex, what happened? Why did you walk into the wall? Were you walking with your eyes closed?"

He didn't answer but just cried.

Later, while we were drawing at the dining table in our room, I asked him again.

"Alex, why did you walk into the wall?"

"*Besser*," he said simply, meaning "better."

I had become overly sensitive to any unusual behavior in my children. Every pain or unexplained fever sent a wave of anxiety through me. I never did find out why Alex walked into the wall. It seemed significant at the time, since I wrote about it in my journal, but it never happened again.

After the kids were asleep in bed, I would go downstairs and chat with some of the other parents from different parts of Germany. The thought struck me that Joseph should have been with us after all. It could have been a chance for us to be together as a family, away from the usual stress. I also felt awkward being the only single parent there.

I couldn't shake the feeling that Joseph was focused more on his own needs. He felt he needed a break from all of us— above all, from the noise and stress of the children. He had applied for rehab for himself, which had been approved for

June. But if Daniela had to undergo a bone marrow transplant, Joseph wouldn't be going to rehab.

I hoped the four weeks we were spending away from him would do him some good. Still, I was afraid that the moment we returned home, he would feel stressed all over again.

During our first rehab in Bad Oexen, I had hoped for the opportunity to talk, to reconnect—but instead, I spent most of the time in the hospital. During this second rehab, we hadn't had the chance to talk at all. Maybe it would allow each of us space to sort out our thoughts. That was the main reason I kept a journal—to go through the thoughts that often plagued me.

I had heard of some husbands who took sick leave so they could be with their ill child or stay home with their healthy ones. Joseph had taken time off in January when Daniela was acutely ill with CMML. But I felt he should take more time off when she went through her bone marrow transplant.

At rehab, another mother told me about a child who had to undergo multiple bone marrow transplants because the first two didn't take. It wasn't until the third attempt that the transplant was successful. The child had spent four months in a sterile tent. Until then, I hadn't realized that more than one transplant might be necessary—or that the entire process could stretch over several months.

The Children's Hospital was building a sterile room in the *Pfaundler* wing, which meant children wouldn't have to be isolated in a tent. But the room wasn't finished yet. And meanwhile, Daniela was getting sicker and sicker.

Alex's Speech

My children were raised in Germany. I spoke to them in English most of the time, but they spoke German with their dad and heard it in kindergarten and everywhere else outside the home. Growing up bilingual, it took them a little longer to form words or speak in full sentences.

When Alex was almost three, he still tended to omit the first syllable of longer words or use the wrong first consonant. The words he used often rhymed with the ones he meant, which was useful to know if you were trying to figure out what he was saying.

Here is a small sample of Alex's vocabulary shortly before his third birthday:

Word:	**Sounded like:**
Gummistiefel (German)	Bummipiefel
chewing gum	pooping bum
Alex	Palace
doch (German)	goch
diaper	biper
grape juice	bape duice
telephone	pevinphone
trinken (German)	kinken
Guten Appetit (German)	Oopen-apip-teet
sauer (German)	fauer
I love you	fuv foo

When Daniela was two and a half, she had a language all her own. She would chatter some kind of gibberish, her face and voice full of expression, as if she were telling a story. I never captured it on camera. I regret that now, because it almost sounded like a real language. I believe in reincarnation (which, for the record, is not part of the Mormon religion). Sometimes I wondered if Daniela was speaking a language from a past life. Without a recording, we'll never know.

By the time she was five, her speech was age-appropriate—mostly in German. But she understood everything I said in English.

Group Consultation

One evening, I took the kids swimming before dinner, so that I could put them straight to bed afterward. But since Alex had napped that afternoon, it took until 8:20 p.m. for him to fall asleep. At 8:30 p.m., I asked the babysitter from the rehab center to check on the children while I attended the group consultation with the doctor.

Thirty-four parents showed up for the discussion. Many topics were covered, but I'm afraid I cast a somber tone over the room when I brought up the topic of bone marrow transplants. I admitted that I didn't know how we could decide whether to move forward with treatment when the chances of survival were so slim. That sparked an intense discussion among the parents, and I was in tears for most of it.

I had just finished reading *Licht am Ende des Lebens* by Betty J. Eadie, the German translation of *Embraced by the Light*. It made me realize that while death is painful for those left behind, it can be a relief for those who have been sick or in pain for a long time. I believed the Lord had a plan for Daniela, but I didn't know what that plan was.

If she were meant to live, I knew I could face the bone marrow transplant with hope, courage, and confidence. But if she were meant to die, no treatment would change that. I didn't want to put her—and all of us—through the agony of a transplant only to have her die in the end.

But I didn't know the Lord's will.

Joseph hoped she would recover without needing a transplant. My faith wasn't that strong—or maybe I was simply being realistic and facing the odds. Unlike him, I was willing to endure anything if it meant she had even the smallest chance of getting well.

The Dream (Tues., April 11, 1995)

I didn't expect the sessions with the psychologist at rehab to stir up so much, but by the third one, I was crying even more than I had in the first two.

I told her about a dream I'd had early that morning. I stood before a wooden bridge, part of it missing—a section had been removed, leaving a gaping hole. Beneath it was a big drop.

The next thing I knew, Alex was hanging in the gap, gripping the wooden beams, in danger of plunging to his death. I watched from one end of the bridge as people crossed from the far side. Then the perspective shifted. I was holding Alex tightly in my arms. I had saved him! My heart pounded with fear at how close I had come to losing him. I wept with relief because he was alive.

The psychologist and I tried to interpret the dream. Did it mean Alex would actually be in danger, and I would have to save him? Why was it him, and not Daniela, that I was so afraid of losing?

That dream haunted me for the rest of the day, leaving me with an uneasy feeling—like a fog that wouldn't lift.

Sauna (Tues., April 18, 1995)

One week later, I took Daniela and Alex to the pool after dinner. Daniela asked if we could go into the little wooden house, meaning the sauna. Although it was reserved for a different group, I checked and found it was empty, so the three of us went in.

We cooled off briefly outside, and I dared to take an ice-cold shower for a few seconds. The kids laughed at my screeching under the cold water.

When we came out of the sauna, the pool was empty, so we enjoyed it all to ourselves. Alex challenged me to chase him around the pool. He sprinted toward the deep end and jumped in—without his arm floats! I rushed toward him. He resurfaced once before I jumped in after him. I grabbed him just as he went under again. He didn't seem scared and hadn't swallowed any water, but I wasn't about to wait around and see what would happen if I didn't pull him out!

That night, Daniela woke up around 1:20 a.m. with an acute earache. The night nurse brought a suppository for pain. I remember how much I hated it when my mom had to give me one as a kid, and there I was doing it with my own child. Daniela put up such a fight that half of the suppository melted in my fingers before I could get it in. Fortunately, I had two more to spare, which was good thinking on the nurse's part.

The pain soon subsided, and Daniela slept until nearly 10 o'clock. When she woke up, she *asked* me if she could go to kindergarten! I looked forward to hearing that question again once we were back home.

Near Drowning (Wed., April 19, 1995)

The next night, we went swimming, and Alex refused to wear his water wings. It was around 8:30 p.m., and there weren't many people in the pool.

I was amazed at how fearless Alex was as he jumped into the deep end without holding my hand. He would jump in, and then I would pull him up from under the water. When we moved to the shallow end, he kept bobbing toward the deep end until the water was above his mouth. I had to pull him back several times.

Then I noticed Daniela standing in the shallow end. She was shaking, even though we hadn't been in the water for long.

"You're not cold, are you?"

Daniela nodded, indicating she was.

"You have to move around to warm up," I said.

Crouching down in the water with only my head and hands showing, I said, "I'm gonna get you!"

I started chasing her. We played four small rounds until Daniela complained again of being cold.

"Go over there and get a towel," I told her.

And then it struck me.

Where's Alex?

I took a quick scan of the pool, counting seven people, but I didn't see him. He wasn't standing anywhere along the edge either.

Panic surged as I started making my way toward the deep end, calling out to the others, "Where's Alex?"

He must be underwater!

Just then, a man standing in the deeper end of the pool spotted a shadow under the surface. He took a few steps in my direction, then lifted Alex's limp body out of the water and carried him to the edge of the pool. A wave of dread washed over me. Alex's face was pale blue as he hung there in the man's hands, seeming lifeless.

I quickly swam to the edge of the pool, my voice shaking as I hollered for someone to call for help. I climbed out of the water, my heart racing, and knelt beside my baby, knowing I had to act quickly.

Daniela was standing next to me, jumping up and down, crying, "*Mein Bruder! Mein Bruder!*" ("My brother! My brother!")

I didn't waste any time. The first thing I did was stick my finger in his mouth to check if it was clear. Of course it was—he hadn't been eating. Then, I gently pushed on his chest. "Does he have a pulse?" I asked the man next to me, my hands trembling, too shaky to check myself. A voice inside me screamed: *He's not breathing! He's got to breathe!*

All those first aid courses I had taken years ago rushed back to me. I lifted his neck, tilted his head back, and blew three short puffs into his tiny mouth and nose. Then I paused.

Three more puffs.

Pause …

Three more puffs.

When he finally coughed, I knew we were getting somewhere. At first, only about a tablespoon of water came up. It wasn't until I continued with mouth-to-mouth resuscitation that he coughed up a larger amount of water. I repeated the breaths one more time, and it was clear that he was recovering. I wanted to scoop him up and hold him in my arms, but a man from the pool suggested I keep him lying down.

I asked for towels, and just then, Alex threw up again—a larger amount of water, along with some of his dinner. By this time a nurse arrived, but she froze at the sight of the scene. I noticed people gathering on the steps beyond the glass windows—spectators—but I didn't have time to think about them.

"Can I pick him up?" I asked, and the nurse nodded. I stood with Alex in my arms and took a couple of steps when he threw up over my shoulder. His belly still felt bloated.

We went into the dressing room, and I stood with Alex under the warm shower. Another nurse arrived to help, taking care of Daniela in the process.

I moved to the bench, wrapped Alex in my big bath towel, and he fell asleep from exhaustion.

Daniela panicked and cried, "Why are his eyes closed? Why is he sleeping?"

I handed Alex to the nurse so she could check his pulse and blood pressure. I wrapped a towel around myself and put

Daniela's bathrobe and shoes on her. We followed the nurse into a nearby examination room, where I saw that Alex's eyes were open. Boy, was I relieved.

"Alex, are you all right?"

"Mm hmm," he murmured softly.

It was then that I remembered the dream I'd had a week earlier. In that dream, Alex was hanging under a bridge—just like floating beneath the surface of the water—and I had saved him.

We not only could have lost Alex, but we could have lost a bone marrow donor for Daniela.

Why did I think that? They had told us from the start there weren't enough matching factors in Alex's blood for him to be the donor.

The nurse came with us back to our room, and another mother showed up as well. The nurse was a huge help, getting Daniela dressed for bed and giving her something to eat. The other mother kept me company with Alex. I was so grateful not to be alone.

I felt Joseph's absence keenly and resented it.

The nurse listened to Alex's lungs again and could hear a faint gurgling.

"The only danger now is that he could develop pneumonia and a fever," she said. "We'll have the doctor check his lungs in the morning."

Once we were sure Alex was stable, the nurse left. A few minutes later, Alex called out, "Mama! *Kinken*!" ("Drink!")

When I brought him his bottle, I smelled chocolate on his breath and asked incredulously, "Did you eat your chocolate egg?"

We had some leftover chocolate from Easter.

"Yeah," he said.

That's when I knew he was back to his normal self.

As for me, I still felt nervous—undoubtedly leftover adrenaline.

How stupid of me. How could I have forgotten Alex?

But on the other hand, I had saved him. I was the one who had gotten him breathing again. Despite my feelings of panic, I did all the right things. I didn't feel proud—I felt amazed and grateful that I had been the one to bring life back into his limp body.

How long had it been?

I replayed the scene with Daniela over and over in my mind, watching the clock, trying to figure out how many seconds—minutes?—Alex had been alone.

When we put him down at the edge of the pool, I never once thought he would die, but I wondered what state he would be in once he was revived. I had no idea how long his brain had been deprived of oxygen.

I had been distracted by Daniela, worried that she was cold. Yet, how awful it was of me to forget about Alex! It made me realize how much of my focus was on Daniela and her welfare.

I thanked the Lord several times that Alex was all right. After he was asleep, I knelt in prayer with Daniela, thanking our Heavenly Father once again.

During the night, Alex coughed and made noises in his sleep. He woke up twice, complaining of a bellyache. When I imagine the trauma Alex must have gone through—how frightened and helpless he must have felt while underwater, gasping for air—I felt his pain and fear.

Neither of us slept well that night.

Back in the Pool (Mon., April 24, 1995)

The day after the near drowning, we tried to go to the clown theater, but they turned us away, saying it was meant for adults and older children.

When I asked Alex if we could go swimming, he said, "*Nein, piefes Wasser.*" (He meant to say "*tiefes Wasser,*" meaning "No, deep water."). I was so upset that he was afraid to —and might never want to again. Combined with being kicked out of the clown theater, I actually cried in front of the children.

As it turned out, a little bit later Alex agreed to swim and to wear his water wings, but Daniela didn't want to go. She sat on the bench and watched us, but after a few minutes, she put on her swimsuit and joined us in the pool.

Alex walked into the pool on his own, and as soon as he was in, he pulled off one of his water wings.

"No, Alex! You have to leave them on. I don't want you to swallow water again."

My inner fear came out sounding more like anger.

Despite what had happened the day before, Alex seemed to have no visible fears. He jumped into the pool and put his head under water. I felt tense and nervous. Each time he dipped his head under the water, even with his floats on, I couldn't help but pull him up.

After Rehab

As if we didn't already have enough illness in our family, Joseph's father had been sick for a while. Six months earlier, doctors had diagnosed him with several small strokes, followed by Alzheimer's disease. After we returned from rehab, Joseph's mother informed us that his father had a brain tumor, which had grown since the scan six months earlier. He could no longer walk and was scheduled to begin radiation therapy that week.

Joseph and his four siblings had a difficult relationship with their father, so their main concern was that their mother would have to take care of him.

Meanwhile, Daniela continued to face her own health challenges. During our time in rehab, she received platelet transfusions once a week. After returning home, she needed two transfusions per week, indicating that her leukemia was getting worse. In March and again in April, she required red blood cell transfusions because her hemoglobin had dropped to 6.2 (normal levels for a child are between 11.0 and 13.7 g/dL). Her platelet count fell to about 10,000 before receiving a transfusion, and even afterward, it never rose beyond 70,000. The low platelets caused her to bruise easily, but these weren't just regular bruises anymore—thick, bulging knots formed under her skin.

Chapter 17

The Search for a Bone Marrow Donor

When I picked up Daniela from kindergarten on Thursday, May 4, 1995, she complained of a headache. On the way home, she threw up in the car. That afternoon, she received her regular platelet transfusion at the hospital, but she was so tired that all she wanted to do was sleep. She drank a little but soon vomited again. I let her rest until Dr. Fischer showed up.

Dr. Emily Fischer was a new, young resident physician training to become an oncologist. She was taller than most of the other female doctors and nurses and always took the time to talk with us or simply listen. After reviewing Daniela's condition, she ordered a chest X-ray. It turned out to be normal, so I got to take Daniela home.

That afternoon, Daniela vomited three more times. The next morning, she vomited twice and continued to complain about her headache. Given her low platelet count, there was a risk of internal bleeding, which could put pressure on her brain and cause headaches and nausea. Dr. Fischer was concerned and had us come in for a CT scan. Even though she hadn't planned to stay long that Friday due to personal commitments, she accompanied Daniela and me to the scan.

Later that afternoon at 2:30 p.m., Joseph and I had sat down with Dr. Zimmermann for a discussion. Dr. Fischer joined us, and when the CT scan turned out to be normal, she expressed her relief.

Dr. Zimmermann gave us an update on Daniela's condition.

"All tests indicate that Daniela's neuroblastoma is still in remission," she said.

Then came the news that offered a glimmer of hope.

"There is a chance of curing Daniela's CMML with a bone marrow transplant. Alex's HLA has one mismatch, but he is still a better candidate than the three potential donors who were tested."

That sounded much more optimistic than before—only one mismatch instead of two, as the doctors had initially believed.

One of the tests, the MLC (mixed lymphocyte culture), came back negative, but the result might not have been inaccurate. Daniela's blood contained very few lymphocytes—a type of white blood cell—that would react with Alex's. There were also too many monocytic cells that suppressed the production of other healthy blood cells. Either there was truly no reaction, or a positive reaction didn't occur because of the composition of Daniela's blood.

Dr. Zimmermann outlined the risks of a bone marrow transplant: one mismatch in the HLA-B locus, a sick child, a child who had already undergone chemotherapy, and a possible recurrence of the CMML or the neuroblastoma.

Joseph asked, "Do we have to decide right now?"

"Of course not," Dr. Zimmermann said.

After blocking Daniela's IV but leaving it in her arm—her veins had become difficult to access, and she was scheduled for more platelets in a few days—we went to the Children's Hospital daycare center where Alex was playing. Normally, Daniela would have wanted to join in, but this time she showed no interest. So, we took the kids home.

By Friday evening, she had vomited two more times, then once during the night. Between 6:00 and 11:30 a.m. on Saturday, she threw up seven times. I arranged for a babysitter to watch Alex until Joseph returned from rehearsal and called the hospital, suspecting that Daniela needed IV fluids.

At the hospital, she was given fluids and electrolytes and slept all day long, waking only for a minute at a time. She ran a low-grade fever (100.4°F / 38.0°C), but her C-Reactive Protein test was negative, ruling out a bacterial infection.

Joseph and Alex dropped by for a short visit. Later, I drove home to pick up Daniela's stuffed animal, Mufasa from the *Lion King*. Daniela was content to have Mufasa in her bed next to Simba and let me go home to sleep.

At home, I kept telling myself, *Tomorrow she'll be awake and in good spirits.* But on Sunday, she slept the entire time.

Dr. Zimmermann stopped by to check on Daniela before leaving for an out-of-town conference on bone marrow transplants with another senior physician. They would be gone for five days, making me feel somewhat anxious—they were the two doctors responsible for the most critical decisions.

After examining Daniela and asking me a few questions, Dr. Zimmermann summoned me out of Daniela's room.

"The longer we wait to find a donor, the sicker she becomes, and the riskier the transplant will be," she said, her concern evident.

We didn't have any more time to waste.

"Has your husband come to a decision?"

I was about to say that we didn't really have a choice—the options were either certain death or a chance to live.

"Yes," I told her. "He agrees we need to do the transplant."

Finding a place for Daniela's transplant was now urgent. The *Kinderklinik* in Freiburg was still renovating a wing of the hospital that would become the new oncology wing, which meant they didn't yet have a dedicated bone marrow transplant room.

Meanwhile, another terrifying possibility loomed. Daniela might have been experiencing an accumulation of abnormal cells in her brain—a condition never before observed among the 110 documented CMML cases in Europe dating back to 1978. However, this was known to occur among patients with AML (Acute Myeloid Leukemia).

Was she implying that Daniela has already entered the acute phase?

I remembered Dr. Zimmermann's warning from January: *If Daniela's condition becomes acute, it will be too late for a transplant.*

She was considering ways to lower Daniela's dangerously high white blood cell count, hoping it would ease her symptoms. There was still a chance that Daniela only had a virus, but she might have been suffering from side effects of her leukemia.

I felt terrible seeing Daniela lying in bed looking so pale, unable to eat or drink, and sleeping all day. I knew, deep down, that something was terribly wrong.

In the afternoon, the doctors started her on 10 mg of morphine over twelve hours to ease her headache. She was also given Zantic (Zantac or ranitidine) to reduce stomach acid production.

I watched the IV drip steadily into her fragile body like seconds ticking on a clock.

When a mother told me that her son was scheduled to begin chemotherapy on June 8 for a bone marrow transplant on June 20, I felt a wave of distress. With only one room planned to be ready for transplant patients, I knew that Daniela couldn't wait for another patient's treatment to finish.

More than anything, I wanted the transplant to be done in Freiburg, with familiar doctors in familiar surroundings. I could sleep at home, and Alex could continue going to his nursery school. If we had to go to a different city, I would either be separated from Joseph and Alex, or the whole family would have to stay in special housing.

I spoke to Dr. Zimmermann about this conflict, and she assured me that she was looking for a place for Daniela to have the transplant. She also mentioned that Daniela might not be able to wait until June to begin.

At night, I meditated with the mantra, *Daniela is going to have a successful bone marrow transplant in Freiburg with Alex as the donor.* I tried to set a date in my mind, but I couldn't. Instead, I added, *Whatever is best for Daniela and all of us will happen.*

At our next meeting, I asked Dr. Zimmermann, "Is there any reason you have to wait until June to perform Daniela's bone marrow transplant here? I mean, are you waiting on special equipment or something?"

"No, everything is here," she said.

A spark of hope lit inside me—maybe they could begin right away. Sensing my optimism, she grinned and said in English, "We'll talk about that on Thursday."

After all my positive thinking, a whole new possibility was opening up in Freiburg.

Since Daniela needed platelets more frequently and wasn't doing well, Dr. Zimmermann grew increasingly concerned about the timing of the transplant. The first bone marrow transplant at the *Kinderklinik* in Freiburg could take place at the end of May, once construction of the sterile isolation room—with proper ventilation and an anteroom—was complete.

Eye Examination

One day, Daniela was using markers to draw on a cloth bag when an ophthalmologist arrived. No one had given her pupil-dilating eye drops beforehand, so we had to wait for a nurse to bring them. Then, we would need to wait another twenty to thirty minutes before she could be examined.

But Daniela refused to let me put the drops in her eyes.

"Mama, is it gonna hurt?" she kept asking.

The ophthalmologist must have grown impatient, because he said, "Let me do that."

With Daniela crying, kicking her legs, and squeezing her eyes shut, he pulled down her lower lid and forced the drops into her eyes.

So much for doctor-patient etiquette.

Mouth Care Mess

While I was doing mouth care with Daniela, she knocked my hand, sending the spoonful of Ampho-Moronal flying. The rust-colored, milky substance splattered all over my new khaki skirt.

I cursed and rushed into the bathroom to scrub at the stain, hoping I was quick enough to prevent it from setting. Since the sun was shining, I laid the skirt out on the windowsill to dry.

When Dr. Zimmermann came in, I had a towel wrapped around my waist, though it was too small to cover everything, leaving part of my leg exposed. She brought me a white lab coat—size small. Normally, it was meant to be worn open, but I had to button it up. It felt tight around my hips.

"It looks sexy," Dr. Zimmermann said with a grin.

That made me laugh.

I got a few funny looks from parents and other doctors, but still wearing my 'sexy' lab coat, I took Daniela to get an EEG. Walking through the hospital, I almost felt like a real doctor—only without the name tag.

Daniela's Condition Worsens

As Daniela's condition worsened, Dr. Zimmermann told me truthfully, "We have a very sick child. If we don't do the transplant soon, she will die on us. Although Alex isn't an ideal match, we can no longer afford to wait for the registry to find a closer one."

I knew it! I had always sensed that Alex would be the donor.

But this meant that Daniela would have to endure high-dose chemotherapy—more intense than the first round—to completely shut down her immune system by destroying her bone marrow, which would then be replaced by Alex's.

Dr. Zimmermann reassured us that she had no intention of giving Daniela—or any other transplant child—a total body irradiation, which was often prescribed as part of the conditioning process. Instead, she planned to use a combination of three different chemotherapy medications to avoid the long-term side effects of radiation in young children. That was a relief.

We also discussed how difficult it had become to insert an IV, since Daniela's veins had gotten stuck so often. She would need a new central venous catheter (CVC) for the bone marrow transplant, which would also make it easier to give her any necessary blood transfusions before the transplant.

Dr. Zimmermann admitted she wasn't sure how well Daniela would recover from the minor surgery of inserting the CVC. The first time she had one implanted—and later removed—she had been in better physical condition.

During those days and weeks, I felt numb. Joseph and I still communicated very little, since we barely saw each other. I spent most of my time at the hospital, while he was either at work or home with Alex. I longed to talk, but Joseph wasn't the kind of person who expressed his feelings easily. So, I held back—maybe to stay strong and keep myself from breaking down. Writing in my journal became my way of processing everything we were going through.

Around that time, I finished reading *It's Always Something* by comedian Gilda Radner, who wrote about her battle with ovarian cancer. The book was published in 1989, the same year that Daniela was born, and the year cancer took Radner's life. An American friend had lent it to me the week before, and I had devoured it.

I often thought about writing a book about Daniela's cancer—something that might help others, but that might help me, too.

Spiritual Guidance

The day before Daniela's CVC surgery, I spoke with our spiritual healer, Angelina.

From what I understood, when Angelina "worked" on Daniela, she would enter a meditative state and envision Daniela with her mind's eye. She would visualize various parts of Daniela's body, cleansing any imperfections she saw, or she would imagine sending white light to help her heal.

When she saw Daniela in person, she held her hands above her, channeling healing energy. She would periodically wipe her hands free of negative energy before resuming, sending warmth and healing vibrations to areas that needed attention—whether it was Daniela's belly, bone marrow, or head.

Angelina also communicated with spiritual guides during her meditation to seek answers. She wouldn't always tell us what she saw or knew, saying she wasn't always permitted to.

"I have to be honest," she told me. "It doesn't look good. Daniela is spending more time on the other side than on this side."

Angelina was right. Daniela had been sleeping most of the time during the first five or six days since she was admitted on May 6.

Referring to Daniela's higher self, Angelina said, "Daniela and Alex have resolved their conflict."

I was afraid that meant Daniela was ready to go.

Angelina told me, "Through the suffering, she will have balanced almost all of her karmic debts."

"What did she owe?" I asked.

"I'm not allowed to be specific," she said. "But it was worth her staying all this time to balance this out. A lot of healing has taken place among all of you."

Can you imagine how I felt? The night before Daniela's surgery—already risky because of her poor condition and dangerously low platelets—Angelina tells me it doesn't look good.

I was so shaken and on the verge of tears, that I had to cancel my chorus rehearsal that evening. There was no way I could stand in front of twenty-two people and conduct. My thoughts were with Daniela, and I felt I needed to be with her, too.

Journal Entry (Mon., May 8, 1995)

Over the past two days I've noticed that when Daniela talks, she uses English. Normally, she answers me in German, even when I talk to her in English, so it's noticeable that she's speaking more English now. The funny thing is, she'll come out with an English sentence five words long! It's in her head because she hears me speak English to her, and she and Alex watch children's videos in English. I only wish she would use English more often. She talks to Alex in German, so he picks up a lot of German from her. He also uses more German words than English, but his sentences aren't as long as those of other German children his age. Still, it seems like he's picked up a lot over the past four weeks.

Daniela's white blood cells were at 132,000 today. Friends often ask me how I cope. Sometimes I cry. Sometimes I yell—usually misguided anger and fear directed at the kids or Joseph. Right now, I'm doing all right. In April, I went through phases of depression and fear, thinking about the bone marrow transplant and all the horrible consequences it could involve.

The Whole Nine Yards

For no apparent reason, Daniela started to feel better and didn't need as many blood transfusions. I felt like calling Angelina again to see what she knew. This time, she was very positive.

"Daniela has the strength and the will to live."

She reassured me that we can move forward with the transplant. She said she would be working on Daniela a lot, so I told her what we should focus on.

I explained that because of the intensive chemotherapy, bone marrow transplant patients often develop painful mouth sores, since the chemo damages the mucous membranes. "That means she could get an infection in her mouth, her esophagus, and all the way down to her butt—the whole nine yards."

Angelina and I burst out laughing at this analogy.

Joseph, who was listening in on my end of the call, had no idea what could possibly be so funny about Daniela's condition.

Later, I tried to explain the pun, but since he's German and had never heard of the expression "the whole nine yards," he didn't get the unintended reference to Daniela's intestines. My dad often used that expression—I bet he would have laughed as much as we did.

I asked Angelina to focus on reducing Daniela's risk of infection as well as the symptoms of Graft vs. Host Disease (GvHD), which all bone marrow transplant patients experience to some degree. With an organ transplant, the body attacks the new organ. But after a bone marrow transplant, the new bone marrow becomes the immune system—and it can attack the entire body. GvHD can cause acute or chronic damage to any organ: lungs, heart, liver, kidneys, and more.

We were all praying and visualizing that Daniela would accept Alex's bone marrow despite the mismatch.

On May 9, 1995, Daniela underwent surgery to receive a new central venous catheter, this time placed in a large vein in her neck. She tolerated the procedure remarkably well—much to the doctor's amazement and our immense relief.

Daniela was always curious about what the doctors were doing. She took after me in that way. Two days after surgery, when Dr. Fischer came to change the bandage on her neck, Daniela wanted a mirror so she could watch. We didn't have one, so Dr. Fischer came up with a clever solution—using the lid of a stainless steel bedpan as a mirror. Daniela held up the lid, looked at her reflection, and could see enough to satisfy her curiosity.

About ten days later, the night nurse told me about an early-morning escapade. At 6:30 a.m., while the nurses were still in shift report, an alarm suddenly sounded. When the nurse rushed into her room, Daniela had unplugged all her machines—including the EKG monitor—and was attempting to make her way to the door with two IV stands in tow.

Daniela had woken up and simply decided she wanted to go for a walk—but that wasn't allowed since she was still in isolation.

High-Dose Chemotherapy (Thurs., May 18, 1995)

Daniela's conditioning—an intensive round of high-dose chemotherapy—began soon after her CVC surgery and lasted for a week. During this time, she was kept in strict isolation. Anyone who needed to see her had to first enter an anteroom, a small room between the hallway and Daniela's hospital room. There, we had to scrub our hands thoroughly and put on sterile gowns before entering her room.

The Cleaning Woman

The cleaning staff was responsible for disinfecting every surface in Daniela's room. They had undoubtedly been briefed on how important this was. One morning, as a cleaning woman was leaving Daniela's isolation room, I spoke to her.

"Good morning!"

"Good morning," she answered.

She wasn't wearing a name tag.

"What's your name?"

"I'm Hannah," she said. "No one here has ever asked me that."

"Thank you so much for taking care of Daniela's room."

"I can't sleep at night," she admitted as tears welled up in her eyes. "I keep thinking about whether I've covered every area of the room. I go over it again and again in my head. I know how important it is to keep it clean."

I was moved by her dedication. "Well, I really appreciate your help, Hannah."

From that day on, whenever I saw her, I made sure to greet her by name. It was the least I could do for someone doing such an important job yet receiving no recognition.

Chapter 18

Bone Marrow Transplant

While Daniela was in the hospital undergoing chemotherapy, we celebrated Alex's third birthday at home with a few of his friends.

Around this time, Alex decided he no longer needed diapers and proudly exclaimed, "Ich bin ein 'big boy'!"

His speech had improved tremendously. He no longer spoke with disjointed syllables or missing first consonants—now he talked up a storm, mostly in German.

Two weeks later, Alex was admitted to the hospital in preparation for the bone marrow donation. His room was on the same ward as Daniela's.

On the morning of Friday, May 26, 1995, Joseph and I rode with Alex in a taxi from the Children's Hospital to the University Hospital Department of Surgery. Though the two buildings were on the same campus and only a six-minute walk apart, we were required to take a taxi for insurance reasons.

I changed into green operating room scrubs, pulling a cap over my hair and holding a mask ready to cover my mouth and nose. Alex clung to Joseph, refusing to let me take him in my arms. We decided he might prefer riding through the patient transfer sluice—a sterile opening with a conveyor system designed to transport patients into the surgical area.

I walked through the recovery room to reach the other side of the conveyor table. (So much for keeping things sterile.)

Joseph placed Alex on the wide conveyor belt, which slowly moved sideways.

When he reached the other side, Alex let me pick him up.

A male nurse took his time in preparing Alex for anesthesia. I set Alex on the table and removed his shirt, sandals, and socks. The nurse showed him the EKG electrodes, which had smiley faces on them, and stuck one on Alex's Winnie the Pooh bear.

"Can I put one of these on you?" he asked Alex.

"No."

Alex's answer was quick and firm.

"What kind of animals do you have at home?"

"Dinosaurs," Alex said. I guess he forgot about our cat.

"Should I draw a dinosaur on here? Tell you what. I'll draw a dinosaur here."

I was still holding Alex in my arms as the nurse sketched something on the electrode sticker. It looked more like a bug than a dinosaur, but Alex must have been satisfied because he let him place it on his back along with two more electrodes that didn't have a bug—I mean dinosaur—on them.

Next, the nurse placed a miniature blood pressure cuff on Pooh's arm.

"Can I put one of these on you?"

Alex nodded. It must not have seemed too threatening.

The nurse even used Pooh's paw for the oxygen and pulse detector, and Alex let him put one on his toe, since he refused to offer a finger. Once the EKG was hooked up, we laid Alex down on the stainless steel table.

The anesthesiologist arrived, and the nurse began to fit Alex for a breathing tube and an oxygen mask. He placed the mask on Pooh's face first, then gently on Alex's. This time, Alex cooperated.

I turned to the anesthesiologist and warned him, "When Alex had an MRI, it took a lot to get him to sleep—drops, two enemas, and two doses of Valium."

An enema is an injection of fluid into the rectum—in this case, a liquid sedative to be absorbed through the bowels.

The anesthesiologist instructed the assistant to start Alex on 8 mg of whatever was in the syringe, but Alex ended up receiving the entire 20 mg, followed by part of a second dose through his IV. Slowly, he gave a big yawn behind the oxygen mask, and his eyes fluttered shut. They didn't close completely like they did when he was asleep but remained partially open, revealing only the whites of his eyes.

The anesthesiologist carefully brushed Alex's eyelashes with his finger. When Alex didn't respond, he said, "He's under."

Through the window, I saw Dr. Zimmermann and recognized her eyes behind round glasses. The rest of her was covered in green except for her hands and forearms, which she held away from her body. I assumed she had disinfected her hands and was ready to be gloved for surgery. Several other medical personnel, also dressed in green, stood nearby. I was struck by how many people were involved in what was considered a small operation.

When I came out, Joseph said, "That sure took long enough."

I told him everything they had done to prepare Alex.

We returned to the *Kinderklinik* and sat in the playroom, talking about anything to pass the time. I'm sure I made a few puns or jokes—partly to keep the mood light, but mostly to calm my own nerves.

Two hours later, I was called into the recovery room. As I walked from *Pfaundler,* I ran into Dr. Zimmermann. She told me the procedure had gone well and that they had aspirated 370 ml of bone marrow from the back of Alex's pelvis—which seemed like a lot for a three-year-old to donate—but that he didn't require a blood transfusion. His hemoglobin had dropped from 13 to 8, but he was given fluid replacement to compensate for the loss in blood volume. He also received a prescription for iron tablets to help restore his hemoglobin levels and support new red blood cell production.

We were greatly relieved that Alex hadn't needed a transfusion. Because of his young age, he hadn't been able to donate his own blood in advance in case he needed a transfusion after the procedure. Joseph's blood would have been a match, but he had taken penicillin for sinusitis until two days before the surgery. Since he was still symptomatic, he wasn't allowed to donate.

There was a slight risk of Alex contracting cytomegalovirus (CMV) or HIV from an unknown donor, so Joseph and I had been hoping and praying he wouldn't need a stranger's blood.

I felt immense relief that Alex's part was over. He recovered quickly from the anesthesia and showed no signs of fatigue or back pain from the procedure.

After Alex and I returned to his hospital room—this time in an ambulance instead of a taxi—I called Daniela on the room telephone. She was in isolation, just two doors down from Alex.

"Is Alex not dead?" she asked, her voice filled with genuine concern.

She had been so worried about Alex giving her his bone marrow. A few days earlier, she had said, "I don't want Alex's bone marrow because then he'll be dead."

I had no idea why she believed that, and I had tried to reassure her that Alex would be fine. But somehow, she must have forgotten. I could only imagine how she must have felt, believing that her brother would die for her.

Joseph and I took turns staying with Alex and Daniela.

Despite the grueling chemotherapy Daniela had gone through, the bone marrow transplant itself was as simple as a blood transfusion. That afternoon, Alex's bone marrow began dripping slowly into Daniela's veins, a process that took six hours to complete, giving us hope that Daniela would soon be able to produce good blood again.

The bone marrow, thick and deep red, looked much like blood in a bag. Yet once inside her veins, it miraculously found its way to her bone marrow, replacing what had been destroyed by chemotherapy.

Daniela made history that day—she became the first child to receive a bone marrow transplant at the University Children's Hospital in Freiburg.

BMT – Day 1 (Sat., May 27, 1995)

The first day following a bone marrow transplant was counted as Day One. Until the new bone marrow began producing blood, Daniela had no immune system and was extremely vulnerable to infection.

As I read *Love, Medicine and Miracles* by Bernie Siegel, M.D., I couldn't help but think of Aaron. His neuroblastoma had returned in January, this time with metastases in his brain. Four months later, he was still alive—but what kind of life did he have? The morphine reduced his pain, but it also kept him asleep most of the time.

Passing by his room, I noticed he was alone. I hesitated, then stepped inside and approached his bedside.

"Aaron," I whispered.

He opened his eyes briefly but closed them again as I continued speaking softly in German.

"You can let go. You are allowed to die. Life is so much better afterward. You won't have any more pain. Your parents will miss you, but they will know you are in a better place. You can go in peace."

I truly believed that.

BMT – Day 3

The day after Daniela received Alex's bone marrow, the doctors began counting the days. By Day 3, Daniela started experiencing side effects from the chemotherapy: rashes across her belly, diarrhea, mouth sores, nausea, vomiting, and a loss of appetite. She began to cough more, and her respiration increased to 50 breaths per minute—well above the normal range of 20 to 27 for a child her age. When her oxygen saturation level dropped to 90%, the doctor placed her on oxygen.

A thin oxygen tube was taped under her nose. Seeing it made me uneasy; it reminded me of the last time I saw Grandma Lizzy.

Daniela tugged at the tape.

"Daniela, you have to leave the tube on. It's helping you to breathe," I reminded her.

She understood but would sometimes pull at it when it itched.

I worried about how she was reacting to the chemotherapy. Even Dr. Zimmermann admitted, "I don't like it."

Daniela didn't have much in her stomach and began vomiting mucus she had been coughing up. We grew concerned about her lungs and the potential for infection.

Alex was no longer allowed in Daniela's room. Dr. Zimmermann explained that young children frequently carry infections, far more than adults, who have already built immunity. Alex—and any other child—had to stay away.

Both he and Daniela were upset when they were told they couldn't see each other, but they talked on the phone from their hospital rooms. I think that helped them both the most.

Daniela looked so sick that it frightened me. Her hair began falling out, little by little. Just days after her transplant, her pillow was covered with strands of blond hair, and her pink scalp was already visible. Friends tried to comfort me. They said it didn't matter if she lost her hair. Maybe it wasn't important— but to me, it made her look even sicker.

BMT – Day 5

The doctors discontinued Daniela's other antibiotics and started her on Imipenem and Acyclovir. She was also receiving Cyclosporine to suppress her immune response. Because a fungus had been detected in her blood, she still had to take Ampho-B.

Daniela's ventilator remained at 50 to 60 breaths per minute, but she didn't need as much oxygen as the day before. She vomited frequently—first mucus, then bile—since she wasn't eating. Despite this, she seemed in better spirits, but she felt tired and slept most of the time.

My mother and two sisters were planning to visit me four weeks later. Olivia faxed a letter filled with words of encouragement, saying she wished they could stay longer than a week but that their visit was a way to show they cared. She rarely signed her letters, but this time, I noticed she had added a special handwritten *'Love, Olivia'* at the bottom.

BMT – Day 6 – Infection

By Day Six, it was clear that Daniela had developed an infection. Her temperature had spiked to 104°F (40°C), prompting the doctors to start her on another antibiotic. She cooperated with her mouth care and took the half tablet of Diarönt (colistin sulfate), prescribed to treat intestinal infections.

When I asked if she felt hot, she said, "Yeah. Should we take my temperature?"

I checked, and it had climbed even higher— 105.3°F (40.7°C).

The nurse gave me a suppository with 500 mg of paracetamol (acetaminophen), but after ninety minutes, her fever had only slightly decreased. To help bring it down, we wrapped her calves in cold, wet towels.

Dr. Zimmermann examined Daniela, who by then had a rash on her chest, belly, back, and right wrist. Her legs looked pale in contrast to the redness on her belly and bottom.

At some point, a photographer came in to take pictures. When I asked why, he explained that the doctors wanted to track any changes, but I never saw him return after that.

The hospital psychologist suggested that Joseph and I go on a date.

I said, "You need to tell that to my husband."

She did, and Joseph later told me that she had recommended we take time for just the two of us at least once a week.

For our first evening out in a long time, a friend from church stayed with Daniela at the hospital, where they watched *The Lion King*. At home, a babysitter put Alex to bed and watched *Star Trek* until we returned after midnight.

Joseph and I went to see *Forrest Gump*. He hadn't heard anything about the movie beforehand and later described it as "a bum becoming a millionaire." It was a great film, but not exactly uplifting while our daughter was in the hospital.

Afterward, we had a delicious meal of calamari and salad. More importantly, we were able to talk a lot. It felt like we hadn't had a real conversation in two and a half years. That night at home, our lovemaking was both intense and deeply comforting.

Despite the psychologist's advice, I don't remember us going on many more dates after that. Between having a child at home and a sick one in the hospital, it was nearly impossible to find the time. We didn't know it then, but Daniela would end up staying in the hospital for seven months straight.

Joseph's father had been a tailor by trade, but with the rise of mass-produced clothing, his work shifted to mending. To make ends meet, he sold insurance—including a hospital benefit policy that covered our children. You never expect to need insurance, especially for a child, but when Daniela was hospitalized, the policy paid us fifty German Marks per day. That money became our lifeline, allowing Joseph to take a year of unpaid leave from the orchestra during the most difficult phase of Daniela's treatment.

BMT – Day 7 – Journal Entry (Fri., June 2, 1995)

Daniela has needed oxygen increasingly since Sunday. In the evening, she weighed 1.5 pounds (700 g) more than in the morning. That means that she is retaining too many fluids. They changed the tube under her nose to a full oxygen mask.

Daniela doesn't look good today. Her cyclosporine level was too low (57 yesterday and 94 today—it needs to be at 300), so the doctors gave her human albumin. A little later, she had fluid in her lungs and wasn't getting enough oxygen. She's already been on oxygen since Sunday, but they had to turn it up to 6 liters per minute. They gave her Lasix to help her get rid of the fluids, and by this evening she only needs about 2 liters of oxygen to keep her at an acceptable level (93%).

She is still breathing fast, about 60 times a minute, and her pulse is also fast at 160. After a couple of doses of Novalgin (metamizole), her fever went down to 99.5°F (37.5°C) around noon today, but this evening it was back up to 101.8°F (38.8°C). Dr. Zimmermann wants her to be without a fever.

Her skin is getting thin from the massive chemotherapy. The rash on her stomach and back is extending down her legs now and itching. She has dark circles under her eyes and looks pretty awful. She feels bad, too, and slept a lot today.

It was a trying day for me, and it went very slowly. It's awful for me to see her suffering.

BMT – Day 8

Daniela had developed a capillary leak, meaning fluids were seeping into her tissues. Using a dialysis machine, they "washed" her blood, removing 800 ml of excess fluid. Her oxygen saturation improved temporarily, allowing them to reduce her oxygen from 14 to 6 liters per minute, but shortly afterward, they had to increase it again to 9 liters.

She needed a lot of oxygen and was slipping into a delirium. Sitting up in bed, she often reached out in front of her or up above her head, as if trying to grab something—or someone? I later reflected on that and wondered if she was seeing spirits from the other side and reaching out to them, wanting to join them.

At night, she couldn't sleep, despite the medications. She was restless and kept fighting with the oxygen mask and calling Alex's name. Blood pooled in her mouth.

I felt utterly helpless. I wished I could relieve her suffering, but all I could do was whisper soothing words.

"The good news is that Daniela has 500 white blood cells," Dr. Zimmermann said, "That means the new bone marrow is starting to produce blood."

It was nice to hear some good news.

Chapter 19

Cardiac Arrest

BMT – Day 9 (Sun., June 4, 1995)

I was at church when I was summoned into the office. Joseph called to say that Daniela was going to be intubated. I quickly found a babysitter from church to watch Alex so I could leave right away.

Despite receiving 15 liters of oxygen per minute, Daniela's blood oxygen saturation remained dangerously low at only 80%. As the doctors sedated her to insert the tube and connect her to a ventilator, she went into cardiac arrest. I arrived to witness the horrifying scene through the window of the anteroom: The anesthesiologist was performing chest compressions while his assistant squeezed a large bag, forcing air into her lungs through the tube they had inserted into her mouth.

I quickly washed my hands, went through the sanitizing process, and pulled on a clean white coat before entering the room.

I leaned against the wall, staring in horror. Around Daniela's bed stood Dr. Zimmermann, Dr. Fischer, another doctor, a familiar nurse, and Joseph. At least she was in good hands. I clasped my fingers to my chest, holding my breath as I watched the doctors try to revive her.

Minutes passed. Finally, her heartbeat returned, but it was very fast, and her blood pressure was weak. Her oxygen levels were still poor. Daniela had been bleeding into her lungs.

They rushed her to the Intensive Care Unit (ICU). Joseph and I ran down the hallway alongside them. At each elevator, someone was already standing there, holding the door open.

How did they know? Did they give some sort of hospital code that I didn't hear?

When we reached an older part of the building, one of the elevators was too small. Without hesitation, the team lifted Daniela from the gurney and carried her upstairs. I remember seeing a nurse carry the empty gurney up the stairs by herself, her strength coming from a surge of adrenaline.

At the top, they placed Daniela back onto the gurney and hurried down the hall.

Once she was in the ICU, they performed a heart echo and took another X-ray. She was given 100% oxygen, but by the evening, they were able to reduce it to 75%.

Another dialysis removed 800 ml of fluid. She received a transfusion of red blood cells and several bags of platelets to help her blood clot.

That evening, I returned my mother's call after listening to her message on my answering machine.

She listened as a concerned grandmother but also as a trained nurse, asking about medical details.

"It sounds like they're doing everything they can," she said, trying to reassure me.

"I know. I just hate that she has to go through all of this," I said.

Later that night, I also called Angelina.

"Daniela left for a short time with all the angels," she told me, describing what she had envisioned. "She was accompanied by a being of light—a guardian—but didn't go out very far. Then she was escorted back with more light from her own being. She's stronger now than when she left. Daniela is very strong-willed. She's a fighter."

"I've always known she was strong-willed. But what do you mean by 'more light'?" I asked.

"We only incarnate parts of our true eternal being. She's bringing back more."

Angelina told me that her spirit guide had instructed her to keep working on Daniela.

That day, two friends from church visited us in the ICU, along with Dr. Fischer and two nurses from the oncology ward. One of the nurses who would have been assigned to Daniela that day said softly, "I liked taking care of Daniela. I'm reluctant to give her up."

As Daniela's condition worsened in the first week following the bone marrow transplant, Joseph and I rented a room in the *Elternhaus*, a housing facility for parents located right next to the Children's Hospital. Families who traveled from farther away could stay there to remain close to their sick child.

The *Elternhaus* (Parents' House), which was newly built in 1995, has since been replaced by a state-of-the-art facility inaugurated in June 2023. It stands next to the new *Kinder- und Jugendklinik* (Children's and Youth Clinic) and is funded entirely by donations to the *Förderverein für Krebskranke Kinder Freiburg* (Support Association for Children with Cancer).

Even though we lived in the same city, we chose to rent a room—not just as a place to rest or retreat, as we told others, but because we needed to be close. We wanted to be able to reach Daniela in minutes if necessary.

That night, Joseph stayed with Daniela until 6:45 a.m. while I slept in the room at the *Elternhaus*.

BMT – Day 10 – ICU (Mon., June 5, 1995)

At 3:00 p.m., Dr. Zimmermann said that Daniela was doing better, but by 10:00 p.m. on the second day in the ICU, she said, *"Es ist ein auf und ab zwischen Hoffnung und Bange."* ("It's an up and down between hope and fear.")

I noted Daniela's vital signs in the evening:

- **Pulse:** 178 (extremely fast)

- **Temperature:** 102.2° F (39.0°C) (still has a fever)

- **Respiration:** 55 (very fast on the ventilator)

- **SaO2:** 95% oxygen level in her blood (while on oxygen)

- **Blood pressure:** 105/32 (68). The diastolic number (the heart's resting state) seemed awfully low to me.

- **Oxygen:** 50% (the concentration of oxygen she was receiving)

Another dialysis removed 560 ml of fluids. In the evening, they began giving her human albumin to increase the volume of blood plasma because her blood pressure was so low. When Daniela first started to have lung problems, the doctors gave her human albumin, and it seemed to make her condition worse, so I was scared when they started giving her more. She also needed a transfusion of platelets every three hours.

Daniela's physical therapist visited her in the ICU with tears in her eyes. A friend from church also came to visit and brought us dinner. After we ate together, Joseph and Alex drove home.

That night, I cried as I left Daniela to sleep alone in the *Elternhaus*.

BMT – Day 11

In the morning, a doctor called me at the *Elternhaus* to say that Daniela was bleeding from her nose. That didn't sound good. I immediately called Joseph at home to let him know.

When I reached Daniela's room in the ICU, the sight was devastating. Blood covered her nose and was splattered across her face, chest, sheets.

I wish Joseph would get here.

She was receiving 100% oxygen, but her saturation was only at 80%. I stood there, speechless and wide-eyed, as the doctor suctioned endless amounts of blood and mucus from her lungs and mouth—several times, again and again.

No one had to tell me. I sensed her condition was grim, confirmed by the steady stream of visitors. The psychologist, Dr. Fischer, and Dr. Zimmermann each came at different times. One of the nurses from the oncology ward checked on her three times that day.

When Joseph arrived, we prayed together—both of us crying, placing Daniela in the Lord's hands if it was His will, yet still pleading for her recovery.

Around noon, they replaced the ventilator, and her blood oxygen rose to 97%, though she was still receiving 100% oxygen. She looked a little better, and the bleeding had slowed. A glimmer of hope returned.

Using a warm, damp washcloth, I wiped the dried blood from Daniela's nose and mouth. She looked much better, and it made me feel useful.

During the course of all this, Daniela developed a fever. It spiked so high that a nurse covered her chest and legs with ice packs to bring it down.

Why bother? I thought, a sinking sense of despair settling over me. I wasn't sure she would make it.

Joseph had lunch with Alex before bringing mine to the *Elternhaus*. After eating, I lay down on the couch and entered the alpha level—a meditative state I had learned through the Silva Mind Control method. My mom had taken the course and highly recommended it, so Joseph and I learned the method when it was offered in Freiburg a while earlier.

Beta waves are present when we are alert, attentive or active, while alpha waves indicate a relaxed state of mind. By using breathing and meditation techniques, we often reached this level to visualize Daniela's healing.

I pictured the bleeding in Daniela's lungs stopping and Alex's bone marrow producing good blood. When I returned to the ICU, I was in much better spirits, and Joseph was astounded.

I leaned close to Daniela and whispered a mantra: "Stop the bleeding in your lungs. The bleeding has to stop. You can stop the bleeding."

I repeated this over and over, and Joseph joined me. I also told her, "Alex's bone marrow is making good blood. It will help you fight infection and clear your lungs."

"Stop the bleeding and cough out the rest," I urged.

Though sedated, I hoped she could hear us on some level.

Two missionaries from the church came to visit. One had once told me that his twin brother had cancer when they were young. Together, we knelt in prayer. At first, they prayed for strength—either to recover or to find peace—but then their words shifted, asking for Daniela's full healing.

That day, Dr. Zimmermann aspirated some bone marrow. Since Daniela was already under anesthesia for the ventilator, she didn't feel the procedure or cry out like before.

The psychologist suggested playing music for her, so I went home to pick up some cassettes. On my way back to the ICU, I stopped by the sibling daycare to check on Alex.

A friend from church called, and another brought homemade Chinese food. It was delicious. We often forgot to eat, so when someone brought us a meal, we were always grateful.

Later, Dr. Zimmermann confirmed the news we had longed to hear: "She's producing good blood—Alex's blood and not Daniela's old blood."

By evening, everyone in the ICU could see how much better Daniela looked. They had grieved with us and now shared our relief. Hope had returned.

BMT – Day 12

Dr. Zimmermann informed me that the doctors wanted to extubate Daniela—take her off the ventilator. Joseph and I were surprised they wanted to do it so soon.

Dr. Zimmermann explained that her oxygen was down to 30% and she was breathing mostly on her own. The ventilator was giving her 20 breaths per minute, while she did the rest herself, totaling 40 to 45 breaths per minute.

The psychologist visited Daniela, and the physical therapist did some breathing therapy with her. I never quite understood how it worked. The therapist placed her hands on either side of Daniela's rib cage and pressed in and out, though she didn't actually move Daniela's ribs.

Dr. Fischer, who had worked the night shift, stopped by in the morning before heading home. In the afternoon, a couple of nurses from the oncology wing came to visit. Even the head of the Children's Hospital, Prof. Dr. Feier, showed up but fussed that there were too many people in the room, scaring them off.

It was touching to see how many hospital staff members were concerned about Daniela's welfare.

After lunch, I ran into Prof. Feier, and we spoke briefly. I mentioned that the doctors wanted to extubate Daniela.

He nodded. "I've already been informed. This will be the first time that I've seen a child oncology patient be released from intensive care alive."

I already knew Daniela was special. Joseph always called her a "power mouse."

At 3:00 p.m., the doctors prepared to awaken and extubate Daniela. A doctor told us one of us should be there when she woke up.

As medical personnel filled the room, another doctor rudely told me I needed to leave. I didn't accept that.

"Someone else can leave if there are too many people here," I said. "If you need more space, I'll move out of the way. Are you trying to spare me something?"

I needed to be with my daughter. No matter how unpleasant the sight might be, I would endure it. I held my ground and stayed.

They reduced the medication keeping her sedated. She stirred, moved her limbs, and coughed. The ventilator was now giving her only 5 breaths per minute—she took the rest on her own.

Then, the doctor discovered that Daniela's central venous pressure and blood pressure were extremely low. As she became more awake, her heart started beating faster. The ICU doctors decided to postpone the extubation until the evening—or more likely, the next day.

Afterward, Prof. Feier's words reverberated in my mind.

This will be the first time a child cancer patient will be released from intensive care alive.

But Daniela was still in intensive care. A chilling question gripped me: *Will she be released alive?*

Joseph, however, was relieved when he heard the extubation had been postponed. He had felt it was too soon. I, on the other hand, felt let down. All that tension, all that nervous energy—expended for nothing. I would have to go through it all again.

BMT – Day 13

Whenever I entered Daniela's room in the ICU, my eyes would scan the machines surrounding Daniela's hospital bed, since I had become familiar with their screens and the meaning behind the numbers. Her fever was down to 36.4°C. Normal. On medication, her blood pressure was stable at 112/58. Her pulse was 112, and respiration was 40. Oxygen was between 45 and 60% with her blood saturation between 95–98%. Overall, this was an improvement compared to the previous days.

Despite this, I felt awful when I first saw how Daniela looked. The previous night, Joseph told me how swollen Daniela's tongue looked. The ventilator tube had to be moved from the right to the left side of her mouth.

I saw how her gums were extended down over her teeth, and both of Daniela's ears were swollen and covered with oozing bubbles. The staff inserted a urinary catheter, and her urine was dark and concentrated. A tube had also been inserted through Daniela's nose down to her stomach and was hooked up to a bag. Dark fluid flowed from her stomach into the bag. Altogether, this was a dreadful sight.

The doctor came to explain Daniela's condition and what she was going through. Daniela had been having seizure activity in her arms and legs at 5:00 in the morning, so they checked her EEG (an electroencephalogram measures brain waves), but it was normal. They increased her Dormicum (midazolam), which was an anesthesia to keep her sedated or asleep. An ultrasound of her bowels showed thickening and significant signs of Graft vs. Host Disease, but at least less blood was being aspirated from her lungs. Her liver enzyme levels were high, and her bowels were affected, as indicated by her stool being yellowish brown and as thin as urine. The doctor had to increase her cortisone.

During those weeks in the ICU, friends came to visit and brought food. Doctors, nurses, and therapists who had treated Daniela in the oncology wing often came by during or at the end of their shift to see how she was doing. Seeing that they all cared was a constant source of comfort for me.

An ICU nurse suggested hanging a photo of Daniela beside her bed, which I thought was a great idea. It would remind the doctors and nurses who she really was, since Daniela's swollen face and puffy eyes, hidden behind an oxygen mask, made her hardly recognizable. The photo would also remind us of how Daniela should look when she recovers and leaves the ICU.

I spoke with the psychologist for a while, and she was fascinated by what Angelina and my mother had shared.

My mother, who had spiritual gifts, told me what she had seen in a vision. She said that in a past life, Alex had been Daniela's mother and couldn't afford to feed her. At six years old, Daniela—then known by another name—wandered the streets of England, begging for food. She perished as a young child.

I spoke with Angelina about this, and she agreed with my mother's vision.

"Alex has paid his karmic debts by donating bone marrow to Daniela in this life."

This made me wonder what it all meant.

"Does that mean that she's going to die?" I asked.

"I'm sorry, but I'm not allowed to divulge that information."

Angelina said that on more than one occasion. She sometimes knew more from her spirit guides than she was allowed to tell.

To help Daniela, I entered the alpha level, envisioning her in my mind's eye and repeated positive affirmations, such as, "Your lungs are getting better and better, clearer and clearer. You're getting better and better, stronger and stronger. You're going to be able to breathe on your own without any trouble. Restore your lungs (your bowels/your skin) to a perfect and healthy condition, like when you were a little baby." And so on.

Daniela received another transfusion of red blood cells to add volume and help increase her blood pressure, since the human albumin tends to leave the bloodstream. She apparently still had capillary leak syndrome. She also received a transfusion of platelets twice a day.

BMT – Day 14

The psychologist met with Daniela each morning at 8:30 during the second week, and I would show up around 9:15.

Daniela was getting better and better. Her blisters had flattened out. Her blood pressure was more stable. Her pulse was down to 100, and she no longer had a fever. She needed only 30–40% oxygen to maintain a saturation of 95%. Respirations were set at 40 times per minute, perhaps to help oxygenate her blood.

No more blood was being aspirated from her lungs—only white to yellowish slime.

The physical therapist came to work with Daniela in the morning. She helped with breathing and moving her limbs. Dr. Fischer and a nurse from *Pfaundler* also came to see her and felt as positive as we did.

The chest X-ray taken in the morning showed improvement.

At this point, Daniela was on the following medications:

- Dormicum (midazolam) 6 ml/hour—for sleep

- Fentanyl 5 ml/hour—for sleep and pain

- Sandimmun (cyclosporine)—a high dose to suppress her immune system and reduce Graft vs. Host Disease

- Amphotericin B—an antifungal medication

- Cyprobay (ciprofloxacin)—an antibiotic for bacterial infections

- A medication to protect her stomach, along with others I didn't remember

Joseph came later and rubbed some cream onto Daniela's skin while I spoke positive words to her as I had the previous night.

I picked up Alex for lunch, and Joseph joined us. We went to the playground together and had a good time riding on the cable slide, playing with a soccer ball, and swinging on the big tire.

Joseph and I went to the parent's lounge near the children's ICU and locked the door from the inside. We knelt and prayed together. A mother of one of the patients showed up and tried opening the door. I got up to open it.

"Sorry," I said. "We were just saying a prayer."

"Are you a priest?" she asked.

"No, we're not," I laughed, feeling a little embarrassed. I wasn't comfortable displaying my faith so openly.

I read to Daniela from *Scripture Stories* and choked up at the story of Abraham being asked to sacrifice his only son, Isaac. I could identify with how he must have felt. Just three days earlier, Joseph and I experienced a couple of hours of hopelessness. We had released Daniela and, through prayer, gave her to the Lord. Perhaps it was necessary for us to show our Heavenly Father that we were willing to let her go—for suddenly, the bleeding in her lungs slowed down, and her condition improved just enough to give us hope again that she would live.

I assisted the nurse with Daniela's care and then retired for dinner and read the local newspaper in the *Elternhaus*.

That night, I did some more visualization, focusing on stopping the T-lymphocyte cells from attacking Daniela's body.

BMT – Day 15

Daniela was doing much better compared to the crisis we went through at the beginning of the week. Her oxygen was reduced to 30%, and she had a blood saturation of 98%. I went home for the first time in six days, and Joseph went to the hospital. We talked on the phone for an hour and fifteen minutes. He told me that her O2 was at 21%, which was the same as the amount of oxygen in the air—a good sign. With oxygen levels at 21%, it sounded like she wouldn't even need oxygen once she got off the ventilator. That would be one less tube. I was eager for that, but the doctors wanted to keep her sedated over the weekend.

She was full of tubes and wires. She had her central venous catheter (CVC) with two lumens (or tubes), an IV in her right arm, another in her left elbow, three EKG electrodes on her chest, and a tube down her nose going to her stomach to remove fluids so that she wouldn't aspirate them. A tube down her throat was connected to the ventilator, and a urinary catheter was in place since she lay in bed all the time. Her hands, feet, face, and eyelids were swollen.

A rectal probe had been constantly measuring her temperature. Thank goodness she was sedated and couldn't feel that! The doctor removed it as soon as her temperature went down because her anus looked sore.

My family called at 11:30 p.m. I talked with my mom, two sisters, and brother-in-law until my father said we had been talking long enough—about forty minutes. It felt good to talk to my family. They were so far away, but a phone call made them seem close. International calls were expensive back then, so we didn't call very often.

Joseph, who was staying at the *Elternhaus*, called me shortly after midnight. We talked until 1:30 in the morning. He asked me whether Alex had used the potty during the day. Alex stopped wanting to wear diapers when Daniela was hospitalized in May, around his third birthday.

I answered Joseph's question but heard no response.

"Joseph? Joseph!" I had to call out his name loudly to get his attention.

"Hmm?!"

Joseph had fallen asleep on the phone.

"Hang up before you lose all your phone time."

We had to buy phone cards with prepaid minutes to use the phone in the room in the *Elternhaus*. It didn't matter whether someone called you or you called them—the remaining time still counted down. That didn't seem fair to me.

BMT – Day 16

The clock radio woke me up along with Alex, who had crawled into Joseph's side of the bed during the night. I made it to church with Alex only a couple of minutes past nine.

At church, a lot of people asked about Daniela. Depending on who I was talking to, I shared either a detailed or abridged version of her condition.

I used to feel like I belonged in the church. But after my daughter was diagnosed with cancer, I felt like an outsider—like an alien. I looked around the congregation and couldn't help but wonder: *Why did this have to happen to me? To my child? Didn't we all believe in the same God? Shouldn't we all receive the same blessings?*

But life didn't work that way. Nowadays, people would sum it up with the simple phrase: *Shit happens.*

Alex and I met Joseph and Angelina at the hospital. Angelina was amazed at how well Daniela looked.

"The lungs are clear," she said as she scanned Daniela with her hands. "The bowels are weak. There's still work that needs to be done there."

Her hands hovered over Daniela, sometimes making sweeping motions. Every so often, Angelina would wipe her hands together and shake them out before continuing to scan Daniela's body.

"Her capillaries look much better." Relief and optimism rang in her voice. "Last week, they were so thin they looked like lace."

That afternoon, I stayed with Daniela in the ICU for four hours. Then I took a break for dinner, provided by friends from church. At 9:40 p.m. I returned to the ICU and learned that Daniela had blood in her diarrhea. The doctor said it could become critical.

I called Joseph and told him. He, in turn, called Angelina. I stayed with Daniela until midnight.

I didn't sleep well, so at 4:00 a.m., I called the ICU nurse to check on her. The nurse said Daniela's blood pressure had been stable since 12:30 a.m. She had received transfusions of red blood cells, platelets, and human albumin, but had more bleeding (100 ml) since 3:00 a.m.

Joseph told me he had received a postcard from a friend that quoted Romans 8:28. I read from Romans 8:24 onward, which speaks about hope:

24 For we are saved by hope: but hope that is seen is not hope: for what a man seeth, why doth he yet hope for? 25 But if we hope for that we see not, then do we with patience

wait for it. ... [28] *And we know that all things work together for good to them that love God, to them who are the called according to his purpose.*
  —*Romans 8:24–28 (King James Version)*

BMT – Day 17

The next morning, I arrived at the ICU early but had to wait until the doctors finished their rounds. While I waited, the hospital psychologist came, and we talked.

I felt really down. At church, I had spoken so positively to everyone, telling them Daniela had made it, that she would be extubated soon, and that she'd be back at Pfaundler by the middle of the week. But now, I wasn't so sure. It felt good to talk to the psychologist, though she worked for the entire Pfaundler wing and rarely had time to meet with me.

I also spoke with the mother of a baby in the ICU. He had been born five weeks premature and had spent the first few weeks of his life in the hospital. Then, at eight or nine weeks, he suffered from sudden infant death syndrome (SIDS). She had been with him when it happened and immediately started breathing for him. In a panic, she ran with the baby to her neighbors to borrow their phone, since she didn't have one. The first neighbor shut the door in her face, saying, "I don't have time right now." The next one helped her by calling an ambulance. By the time paramedics arrived, her baby had been clinically dead for ten minutes. She had been giving him mouth-to-mouth resuscitation that whole time while his heart was not beating.

He suffered acute kidney failure, but she told me they were functioning again. She was overjoyed that he had survived.

"I don't know if he has any brain damage," she said, cradling her baby in her arms. "It doesn't matter to me if he does. He's my baby, and I love him."

I couldn't help but think that it *would* matter to me if my child were brain-damaged.

To my surprise, one of the doctors told me they were going to reduce Daniela's medication (fentanyl and midazolam) to allow her to wake up so they could remove the ventilator tube. As it turned out, she didn't wake up as much as they had hoped, but she was breathing partially on her own. Her blood pressure was stable, but it had been low the previous night. They gave her two transfusions of red blood cells—once at midnight and again at 11:00 in the morning—as well as some platelets and human albumin. In the late afternoon, the doctor told me that rather than extubate her in the middle of the night, they were going to wait until nighttime to turn off her sedatives so that she would be awake by morning.

Exhausted, I went to bed around 8:30 p.m., sleeping in my clothes in case I received a call that Daniela was waking up.

No one called.

Joseph talked to Angelina again. She said she had located the source of the bleeding—where the small intestine enters the large intestine. It reassured me to know the bleeding was confined to one area rather than occurring throughout her intestines, as the doctors had feared. Angelina didn't seem worried about it and was actively working on healing it.

It was shocking to see the thin, blood-tinged liquid coming from Daniela's bowels. The first time I witnessed it in the ICU, I gasped, "Oh, my God!" This time, however, Angelina's soothing words helped ease my worry.

Angelina advised us not to tell Daniela to *stop* the bleeding, as it might serve a purpose. Instead, she suggested we encourage healing by saying, "Restore your bowels" or "Regenerate your bowels to be healthy."

I took her advice and began repeating, "Daniela, restore your bowels to a perfect and healthy condition."

BMT – Day 18 – Extubation (Tues., June 13, 1995)

The doctor informed me they were going to remove Daniela's endotracheal tube that day. Joseph and I tried to wake her up. We laughed and made jokes, hoping to ease the transition for her while also relieving the tension we had felt ever since the doctors first mentioned extubation and liberating her from the ventilator.

At 11:25 a.m., the tube came out easily. Daniela coughed and began breathing on her own. We all felt as though we had witnessed a miracle.

The physical therapist came twice to help her with her breathing. However, around 1:30 p.m., Daniela's breathing increased from 50 to 70 respirations per minute and became labored. At 3:00 p.m. she was given a pain reliever. By 6:00 p.m., she was still breathing rapidly, but it was less strained. Then, as more mucus accumulated, she coughed it up, letting out groaning noises. Her pain medication was switched to Dilantin (phenytoin), a stronger drug that I later learned was actually an anti-seizure medication.

We assumed Daniela was experiencing abdominal pain, as she was still bleeding from her bowels. The nurse told me that the previous night, Daniela had lost 200 ml of blood in one hour, but that evening she had lost only 100 ml in two hours, indicating that the bleeding was slowing down. I felt relieved to hear that.

I had lunch with Joseph and Alex, then they took a nap in the *Elternhaus*. Alex sounded hoarse and was probably coming down with something. Joseph had planned for him to visit Daniela, but the doctor said it wasn't a good idea—confirming what I had already told Joseph. So, he took Alex home, saying he wanted to return between 7:00 and 9:30 p.m. But when he called at 8:30 p.m., I told him it was too late to relieve me. I felt irritated that he hadn't come sooner.

I stayed with Daniela until 10:20 p.m., reading a church magazine. She never fully woke up—never opened her eyes—but she moved her arms, legs, and head slightly.

Angelina called at 10:45 p.m., and I told her that the bleeding seemed darker and less frequent.

"I feel her large intestine is getting better," she said. "Her lungs look much better, too."

"I thanked the angels in prayer today."

"That's so important. They need to feel our love."

"Angelina, did these spirits once have a body?"

"No, they're following a separate path of evolution. They never had a body, and they never will."

I found that fascinating. As a church member, I adhered to its teachings, but I never gave up my belief in reincarnation, spirit guides, or angels.

BMT – Day 19

I arrived at Daniela's room as the doctor lifted her to be weighed. Daniela opened her eyes a little and stretched her legs. Her weight showed she was still retaining too much fluid.

When Daniela was back in bed, she opened her eyes again but didn't focus on me. Her eyes crossed a little as she gazed upward or far to the left.

In the afternoon, her breathing made gurgling sounds, and every three seconds or so, she would open her mouth wide, stretch her head back, and tighten her right hand, pulling her arm up. After a while, she began to accompany these repetitive movements with slight groaning sounds.

The doctor and the nurse thought Daniela was in pain. They started her on Tramal in an IV solution. When that didn't seem to help, they gave her Dilantin. She calmed down after thirty minutes, but it only lasted about two hours.

I kept wondering, though, if Daniela was maybe having withdrawal symptoms from the narcotics and painkillers. I didn't want to believe that she might be having seizures.

Joseph showed up at 8:40 p.m. after work. We talked for an hour. Then I went home and talked to Sister Bachmann. She was from Bern, Switzerland, and was serving as a senior missionary for the Mormon church. She was unmarried and probably in her mid-fifties. She had short hair, wore thick-framed glasses, and was dressed in a white blouse with a dark skirt. She came to help us with housework and with Alex and was going to stay for about a month.

I wasn't sure what to think of her yet, but I appreciated the help.

Chapter 20

Transfer from the ICU

BMT – Day 20 (Thurs., June 15, 1995)

At home Alex woke me up at 1:00 a.m. I had to refill his bottle three times throughout the early morning hours. His hoarseness was now accompanied by a fever, which reached 102.2°F (39°C). Ever since Daniela's illness, I became anxious whenever my children had a fever—this time was no exception.

I rearranged the office furniture so that Sister Bachmann could sleep there. We had a sofa that could convert into a bed.

For lunch she prepared curried chicken and rice, along with a salad made with Chinese cabbage.

As we sat down to eat, Joseph called to say that Daniela was being transferred from the ICU back to the oncology wing. I couldn't believe it was happening so soon. I arrived at the hospital just in time to help with the move and carry our belongings to Pfaundler.

I spoke with one of the senior physicians. He was a skilled technician—if someone struggled to insert an IV, he could do it. However, where he excelled in practical work, he lacked in doctor-patient etiquette. He always made everything sound grim. When discussing Daniela's condition, he said, "We are cautiously optimistic." That seemed to be his approach with all his patients—though more cautious than optimistic. I much preferred talking to Dr. Zimmermann. She was intelligent, well-educated, and professional, yet her demeanor was soothing. Even when delivering bad news, her words were always kind.

I called Angelina to share the news about Daniela's transfer. Later, the physical therapist came to work with Daniela in her new room at Pfaundler.

Joseph left for work in the evening and returned at 10:20 p.m. with ice cream. How sweet of him.

BMT – Day 21 – Back at Pfaundler (Fri., June 16, 1995)

When I entered Pfaundler on Day 21, it pained me to look into Daniela's eyes and see them never meet mine. She often had them open, but they never focused on me or anyone else. Her pupils were dilated and unresponsive to light. No one could say what that meant.

The neurologists performed an EEG, and later I heard that it was good—her brain activity changed when her eyes were open versus closed, which was as it should be.

Daniela kept opening her mouth and stretching her head back, as if trying to clear mucus from her throat. She bent her wrists inward while straightening her arms. My first thought was that she looked physically or mentally disabled.

The doctors were as shocked as I was. They said it could be a result of prolonged sedation in the ICU and the trauma her body had endured—that it might take several weeks to recover.

But it could also be due to pressure in the brain—either through swelling or bleeding into it. No one could say yet whether she would recover completely or suffer lasting impairment.

Can you imagine how I felt? During her CPR three weeks earlier, I had prayed, *If she's going to be brain-damaged, take her now. Don't let her come back.*

We wanted Daniela to fully recover or for the Lord to take her. The state she was in just couldn't be permanent. That would be an absolute tragedy. Ever since the senior physician spoke to me about it, I felt down. He had a way of delivering news so negatively that I couldn't help but feel pessimistic about her chances for recovery.

A short talk with Angelina lifted my spirits a little.

I also spoke at length with the hospital psychologist and ended up crying. Later, Dr. Fischer told me I needed to get some sleep, do something for myself, or go out with Joseph.

I left the hospital around 7:30 p.m. and went shopping. Mostly, I looked for cleaning supplies—not exactly doing something for myself, but at least it was a change. I would have bought more food, but by then it was close to 9:00 p.m.—closing time.

One of my adult piano students called and asked how Daniela was doing. I told her, then asked about her baby girl.

"She's great," she said. "Our easiest baby."

My throat tightened as I held back tears.

"How is Joseph doing?" she asked, breaking my silence.

"I don't know, really."

I'm sure she heard my voice shaking.

The truth was, while I was open with my feelings, Joseph rarely shared his. At one point, he was so enraged that he shook his fist at the sky and exclaimed, "I am so angry with him!"

That scared me. Neither of us could understand why our daughter had developed cancer. If Joseph was angry at God, would he lose his faith?

For me, my beliefs helped me survive the hardest moments. I held onto hope that Daniela would recover. If I let go of that faith, I felt I would have nothing left to cling to—nothing to help me cope.

BMT – Day 22

Alex woke me up at 7:00, but we didn't get out of bed until 8:00. I baked some peanut butter bars for the Pfaundler wing, while Alex and I watched some videos.

I tried to call Joseph at 11:15 a.m., but a nurse told me he was in the *Elternhaus*.

"How is Daniela doing?" I asked her.

"Not good. Worse. She needs oxygen again, and she's having more seizures. Can you come?" At 4:00 a.m., the night nurse had called Joseph in the *Elternhaus*, because Daniela's small seizures suddenly increased in strength.

Seizures. We finally had a word for those strange movements she had been making. I was so upset that I started to cry.

I managed to get a babysitter on the phone and asked her to take care of Alex. She came over as soon as she could, so that I could go to the hospital.

When I saw Daniela, she didn't look all that bad—about the same as the day before.

Dr. Fischer ordered an ophthalmologist to examine Daniela's eyes. He said she definitely had papilledema— swelling of the optic disc—most likely caused by increased pressure in the brain.

Angelina came to visit Daniela. When she entered the room, she looked at me but then looked at the space around my body, scanning my aura again to see how I was doing. She did that with everyone she worked on.

"When Daniela is out of her body," Angelina said, "she is afraid to come back, but she still has some healing to do between herself, Joseph, and you."

After working on Daniela, she sat down with Dr. Fischer and me. Angelina told Dr. Fischer what she had seen over the previous two weeks, including the time when Daniela left during her cardiac arrest on June 4th.

"She was brought back accompanied by an angel or being. I've never seen anything like it. I even took notes on it," she said. "Her lungs are much better. She had fluid throughout her lungs, but now it's only in her upper chest. She had bleeding in her bowels between the small and large intestines, but this has improved over the past few days."

I was impressed that Dr. Fischer was so receptive.

When Dr. Fischer left, Angelina told me, "She's lovely. You're in good hands."

Angelina noticed something on the left lobe of Daniela's brain. A week earlier, she had seen two lesions that were no longer there. What she saw now appeared diffused and somewhat dull. She worked on it and said it would improve within a few hours. She felt we should wait on a CT scan, suspecting it wouldn't reveal anything.

Angelina also noted that Daniela's right kidney was underperforming more than the left. Her heart was under stress, which was linked to her kidney issues. Angelina said the increased swelling in her eyes was also related to her kidneys.

While the eye doctor had detected eye pressure in the morning, a CT scan in the late afternoon showed no fluid accumulation in the brain.

Before I left the hospital, Dr. Zimmermann gave me an update.

"The CT shows nothing new, but we still have a child who isn't awake."

"Do you think she has brain damage?" I asked, afraid that voicing my fear would make it real.

"At this point, we don't know what her cognitive state will be when she fully wakes up. I can't say whether Daniela will graduate with straight A's or be severely intellectually disabled."

After the CT scan, I went home, put Alex to bed, and called Angelina. We talked for almost an hour.

I asked Angelina about Dr. Zimmerman's concerns. Angelina's counselor—the heavenly being she communicated with—assured her there was no damage. Sometimes they withheld certain information, like in the case of a 40-year-old pregnant woman who wanted to know if her baby had Down syndrome. But whenever Angelina received information, it had always been true.

"I've never been lied to," she said.

That reassured me. At the end of our conversation, she said we need to have patience, predicting Daniela would come back in about three days—Tuesday or Wednesday.

"But don't be upset if it's later. I'll look at it again."

That night, I returned to the hospital to relieve Joseph, who went home so he could take Alex to church the next day. I stayed with Daniela until 12:45 a.m.

Around midnight, the senior physician came in to check on her. As he spoke, I held three fingers together, relaxed my body, and repeated positive thoughts in my mind. This time, his report didn't unsettle me. I felt comforted—both by my relaxation techniques and by what Angelina had told me.

Alex seemed to have adapted well to the routine of living with one parent while the other stayed with Daniela at the hospital. Ever since he was a baby, his sister had been in and out of the hospital. It had become our way of life—though certainly not one I would have chosen for any of us.

Whenever I was with Alex, I did everything I could to make him feel secure, showering him with love. I also spoiled him with gifts. That was my way of compensating for what he couldn't have, like a healthy big sister.

BMT – Day 23

For the first time since developing papilledema, Daniela's pupils reacted to light. Her respiration slowed from 42 to 32 breaths per minute and became more regular, and her pulse remained at 130.

She even showed slight reactions when I spoke to her. When I told her that Alex was outside the door, looking at her through the glass, she squirmed a little, and her eyes moved beneath her eyelids.

A nurse and I assessed Daniela using the Glasgow Coma Scale. She scored between 10 and 11 points—where 3 is the lowest and 15 the highest. A score of 11 was the minimum for a "relatively good prognosis."

Until then, I had described Daniela as "asleep" or "not awake," but I hadn't considered that she was actually in a coma. Finally, I had a name for Daniela's condition. She was in a comatose state.

I didn't know whether her cardiac arrest had deprived her brain of oxygen or if the trauma from her severe Graft vs. Host disease was the cause—likely, it was both. The uncertainty of her full recovery was terrifying. Talking about it with Joseph or anyone else would make it feel too real, so I chose to keep my fears to myself. It was my way of coping.

Angelina called to say she was still working on Daniela's brain. It was improving, but she could only work on it for twenty minutes at a time, as it needed a few hours to show progress.

Friends often asked me what I did all day long. I would help move Daniela to a new position every two hours, change her diaper, clean her mouth, and apply cream to her dry skin. Sometimes, I would read something or write in my journal.

After spending so much time at the hospital, being home felt strange. I no longer worked for the network marketing company. I preferred staying by Daniela's side, where I could monitor her condition and be there for her.

BMT – Day 24

I was watching a movie on television when Joseph called and asked me to come home. It was the first night we had spent together at home in over two weeks, and we made good use of it!

By morning, Alex's fever had subsided, and his cough was mild, so I took him to his playgroup. I spent the rest of the morning with Daniela until lunch. Joseph picked up Alex on his bike, met me for lunch, put Alex in the sibling daycare, and then stayed with Daniela while I went home. I wasn't sure what to do with myself, so I took a much-needed two-hour nap.

When I returned at 4:30 p.m., Joseph met me at the door and said, "Daniela's awake! She's pretty much here!"

I felt my chest swell with excitement, but by the time I washed my hands, got Alex ready, and received permission for him to enter, Daniela had fallen back asleep.

Joseph described how her eyes had been wide open. She had looked at the physical therapist and even reached out to her with one hand. The therapist had been moved to tears.

I felt a pang of disappointment. I had waited so long to see Daniela's first signs of awareness. But we would have to wait a little longer. The emotional highs and lows were exhausting.

After dinner, Joseph took Alex home. For nearly two hours, I sat in a lawn chair with Daniela on my lap. We listened to a CD of Bach flute and organ music—Angelina playing the flute—while I talked to Doris on the phone.

Daniela's blood pressure remained high, which seemed strange, since only a week before it had been too low. They gave her Adalat under her tongue up to four times a day to lower it, and she had already needed it three times that day. Her pulse fluctuated between 90 and 140, mostly settling between 120 and 130.

When I arrived, I noticed a different nurse caring for Daniela.

"What happened to the other nurse—the one who rubbed Daniela's skin with moisturizing cream?" I asked.

"She was assigned to Daniela, but it got to be too much for her. She was sent home. She has a week off now anyway."

I had noticed two days earlier that the other nurse had tears in her eyes. Seeing Daniela in a coma had been too difficult for her.

For us as parents, it was often too much as well—but there was no one to relieve us. We had to stay strong and keep showing up. *It builds character.* Grandma Lizzy's words often rang through my head. I was willing to be strong for my daughter. It became part of my character. Or maybe it had been there all along.

That night, I asked another nurse how she was holding up. She admitted that, even after hearing about Daniela's condition beforehand, seeing her like this had been a shock. But over time, she had gotten used to it. I realized I had, too. That didn't mean I wanted Daniela to stay this way. I kept looking for signs of improvement.

She was taken off the oxygen for several hours and did fairly well with a saturation of 94%.

The doctor performed an ultrasound of her liver, kidneys, and bowels. Her regular Monday morning chest X-ray—taken with a portable machine—had already been done before I arrived.

She was also hooked up to an EEG, which recorded her brain activity for several hours and overnight. The neurologist, a specialist in brain, nerve, and spinal cord disorders, later confirmed there were no signs of seizures—only muscle movement. A sonogram of the blood supply to her brain, taken through her temple, also looked normal, aside from showing her elevated blood pressure.

BMT – Day 25 (Tues., June 20, 1995)

After spending the morning with Daniela, I went to the cafeteria for lunch. About half-way through my meal, fifteen children, aged eight to eleven, entered. They were from Chernobyl, where the catastrophic atomic disaster occurred in 1986. They had been brought for medical tests and possible treatment.

I said hello to one girl who looked about ten or eleven years old. She paused at my table.

"Ummm," she said, looking up at the ceiling. "*Gu-ten Appe-tit.*"

She had to think about how to wish me a "good appetite" in German.

"*Danke schön!*" I said.

She grinned, proud of her success.

It was fun to connect with them and make them feel welcome. They were offered some cold lemon tea to drink, but after a few hesitant sips, some of them said, "*Nyet.*" Then they were served bottles of apple juice, which they liked much better. I 'oohed' and 'aahed' with them.

I suppose any child would prefer apple juice over lemon tea. I felt grateful that these kids were finally receiving care they couldn't get at home.

Later, Angelina came to work on Daniela for half an hour.

"She's much better," she said. "She may come back soon—but not before tomorrow."

"Do you think it will happen suddenly or gradually?"

"It could happen quickly. I'm not sure." She had to rush off to teach a class but added, "I'm really happy about her."

That afternoon, I told Daniela's nurse, "You're about to experience something wonderful."

She looked at me puzzled. "What?"

"Daniela's coming back soon."

As I spoke, I felt a brief but strange surge of energy in my head and upper body. *Should I not have said it?*

But the nurse shivered. "That gave me goose bumps all over."

Joseph relieved me at the hospital, so I could return home before dinner. It was sunny and hot for the first time all year. When I got to the apartment and found it empty, I looked down from our fourth-floor balcony and saw Sister Bachmann with Alex in the sandbox. I was grateful to see Alex playing in the sand without any worries.

That evening, I invited two missionaries over for dinner. Sister Bachmann fixed a large salad for us. When I heard that the missionaries were heading to church afterward to play volleyball, I decided to join them—I could use some physical activity. I wasn't great at volleying, but I had a strong serve and managed to score a few points.

When I got home, Sister Bachmann was watching *Ghost* with Patrick Swayze, Demi Moore, and Whoopi Goldberg. After calling Joseph, I watched the rest of the movie with her. I had seen it before—it was probably my favorite, with its perfect mix of suspense, humor, romance, and spiritualism.

Earlier that day, Doris had stopped by, and we chatted outside Daniela's room. She hadn't worked for us in a while, but we had stayed in touch. Our shared American background kept our friendship going. She had come directly from the dentist. Her mouth was sore and numb and made funny movements, giving her a crooked smile.

She lent me a book called, *Your Guardian Angels: Use the Power of Angelic Messengers to Enrich and Empower Your Life* by Linda Georgian. I started reading it when I went to bed. I couldn't put it down until well after midnight.

BMT – Day 26

When I took Alex to his daycare, it was the first time he clung to my leg, clearly not wanting me to leave. With Daniela in the hospital, Alex wasn't getting much time with me, and each time I had to leave him, I felt a pang of regret in my stomach.

During the morning, I carefully peeled the dried, loose skin from Daniela's left palm and from under her fingernails. As a kid, at school I used to love rubbing white glue on my palm, waiting for it to dry, and then peeling it off like a layer of skin. That's exactly what this felt like—except this was real skin, a side effect of the Graft vs. Host disease.

At lunchtime, I ran into the neurology specialist and asked if he had a diagnosis or prognosis for Daniela. He said he would be happy to talk with me but preferred to do so with the other doctors present, so that we would all receive the same information.

In the late afternoon, after Daniela had spent about an hour and a half lying on my lap in the lounge chair, I put her back in bed. At 6:00 p.m., the neurologist arrived, and we met with Dr. Zimmermann and Dr. Fischer in another room.

The neurologist confirmed that the stretching or tonic movements Daniela was making were *not* seizures.

"Daniela is comatose, but she's now in a recovery phase, much like a child in the neurology ward who has suffered a head injury or drowning incident," he explained. "However, she is showing some neurological improvement."

"Do you think her recovery will happen quickly?" I asked, hoping for a reassuring answer.

"Some parents think when their child is asleep, it will suddenly wake up. But it's not like in the bible where the child just stands up—it's a gradual process. Every day, they improve a little bit."

"Have you ever seen a child come back suddenly?"

"No, I haven't," he admitted.

That was discouraging.

Her recovery could take days, weeks, or even months. No one could predict how long it would take or whether Daniela would fully recover, but we always held on to hope. We tried to will it into reality through prayer and visualization.

Joseph stayed with Daniela at the hospital while I went home to put Alex to bed. To my surprise, he was already there, and I was happy to find him still awake. I brought him a bottle or two, then watched him drift off to sleep.

Later, I returned to the hospital to watch a video with Joseph called *Made in Heaven*. The premise—two spirits who fall in love in heaven must find each other on Earth—seemed interesting, but the way it was done was odd. We both thought the film's version of heaven was too earthly, especially since one of the "heavenly bosses" smoked and had a twitch.

That night, we both slept at the *Elternhaus*, but I felt so tired that all I wanted to do was sleep.

BMT – Day 27

Joseph and I slept through the alarm. He suddenly jumped out of bed, because he had to get to work. Since Daniela was no longer in acute danger, we decided to give up our room at the *Elternhaus*. I packed everything and spent some time with Daniela.

Joseph returned after a short rehearsal, and we loaded the car. I stripped the beds and returned the keys with a sense of relief. It felt good knowing that Daniela was out of immediate danger.

While Joseph stayed with Daniela, I went home for lunch with Sister Bachmann and Alex. Afterward, the three of us took a nap. I was rudely awakened by the sound of a horn—Joseph had come home for an hour to teach a young horn player, leaving Daniela with the nurses.

While I found the sounds of a student horn player to be annoying, they apparently weren't enough to wake Alex. I had to rouse him myself to take him to an appointment with a speech therapist. At three years old, Alex's speech was not as developed as other children his age. He often left off the first consonant of words and rarely formed complete sentences.

The therapist tested him by showing pictures and asking him to name them. After twenty minutes, his attention waned, and he wanted to go home.

She determined that Alex had all the necessary sounds for speech. While he couldn't say the initial *sh* sound in *shopping*, he could say *fish*, which reassured her. She felt he was too young for therapy and suggested we return in nine months if we still had concerns. I wasn't too worried—I figured he just needed time to sort things out since he was growing up hearing two different languages.

At one point, my German mother-in-law asked, "Why don't you just speak to him in German?"

I raised my eyebrows in disbelief. "If he doesn't learn English, he won't be able to talk to his American grandparents!"

I'm glad I stuck it out speaking English with Alex, because eventually he caught up and became fully bilingual.

Joseph didn't seem to have strong feelings about it. I often encouraged him to speak more English at home, since the kids heard German everywhere else. He would start speaking in English but would slip back into German after a few sentences. Then again, after living in Germany for a total of eleven years, my German had improved to the point where it was probably better than his English—so maybe he just felt more comfortable speaking German with me.

It was a long Thursday—when stores stayed open until 8:00 p.m. instead of the usual 6:30—I went shopping for clothes and shoes for Alex, taking a break to treat us to some ice cream. I felt kind of strange pushing a baby stroller through town, since I hadn't done it in such a long time.

Olivia called me at midnight to ask about the weather for their upcoming visit. My mother and two sisters were coming to visit us for a week at the end of June. I told her to be prepared for hot, cool, or rainy weather—everything except snow. That's how the weather seems to be in Germany for three out of four seasons of the year.

BMT – Day 28 (Fri., June 23, 1995)

It had been four weeks since the bone marrow transplant. Some bone marrow recipients were released from the hospital in six to eight weeks, but we still didn't see an end in sight for Daniela's stay.

Joseph was drained from being in the hospital for two days. Since he had a rehearsal in the morning, it was my turn to be with Daniela. He also wanted to prepare our tax report in the afternoon, so I ended up spending the whole day at the hospital.

As always, I helped the nurses, this time assisting with a "system change"—replacing all the IV lines connected to Daniela's central venous catheter.

I wrote in my journal and read from the book Doris lent me, *Your Guardian Angels*. The physical therapist worked with

Daniela for an hour after lunch. Afterward, I sat in a chair with Daniela on my lap while her mattress was exchanged for a special orthopedic air mattress. At first, the pump sounded like a vacuum cleaner, but after several minutes, it settled into a tolerable whirr, a little louder than central air conditioning. The air flow shifted the mattress's pressure points, helping to prevent bed sores.

I took another break to eat some strawberries. Doris called me in the room, and we talked for an hour while the nurse bathed Daniela and rubbed cream on her body.

The nurse also had to give Daniela the contents of a corticosteroid capsule (Budenofalk) for her bowels. Since Daniela had a feeding tube in her nose that extended down into her stomach, the nurse pulled apart the capsule, poured out the tiny beads, mixed them with liquid, and squirted them down the tube. The first time she did it, I praised her for her technique, because it went so smoothly. But this time, using the same technique, the tube got clogged, and the tiny white beads wouldn't move in or out. It took the nurse at least fifteen minutes to get them all down the tube. What perseverance she had!

BMT – Day 29

Alex woke me up at 7:00 a.m. with an apple in his hand that had one small bite taken out of it.

"I wann' eat apple."

I got up to cut it for him. He ate some, then we lay back down while he drank a bottle of milk. We slept for another two hours until Joseph left for his rehearsal, and I went to the hospital.

Dr. Zimmermann came to look at Daniela's bottom, which was getting sore from the constant diarrhea she was having. She was suffering from Grade 4 Graft vs. Host disease in her bowels. Her kidneys were better and had a normal creatinine level, but her liver was still affected, showing a bilirubin around 8 mg/dL. (A normal level of total bilirubin is 0.1 to 1.2.) The whites of her eyes were still yellow and bloodshot.

The nurse rolled Daniela onto her stomach on an open diaper so that her bottom could air out. During that time, Daniela was lying with her head turned to the left. I noticed she was becoming restless and making chewing movements. In less than a minute, she had chewed the inside of her right cheek until it was open and bleeding. Just two days earlier, she had done the same to her left cheek. I felt so bad for her every time things like that happened. I also felt helpless to stop them from happening.

I read several stories from the angel book out loud to Daniela. I also felt I should play some home videos from before Daniela's bone marrow transplant, so I watched the video of Alex's birthday. Daniela seemed to react to the voices by moving her head often and breathing faster.

For a few days, the nurses stopped giving Daniela Adalat when her blood pressure went above 130/80. I was glad. It always caused her pulse to go way up. When she rested, her blood pressure was good at 124/67, but when she was restless or excited, it was around 147/95.

I was often plagued by dreams. I would dream that Daniela was awake and running around, and I felt overjoyed that she had fully recovered.

Then I would wake up, and reality would set in.

BMT – Day 30

Joseph and I had difficulty getting up. When Sister Bachmann, Alex, and I left for church at 9:15 a.m., Joseph was still in bed. He got up later and went to be with Daniela. Getting up in the morning had become increasingly difficult. On Sundays, when we wanted nothing more than to sleep in, making it to church on time was a struggle. It was easier to use the hospital as an excuse than to show up late to church.

Alex was uncooperative. When I brought him to the church nursery, he wanted to leave. We went back to the car to get his bottle, which I had to fill with water since I had forgotten to bring juice. When we returned to the nursery, I got him some Duplos to play with, and then I was able to go to Sunday school for the last five minutes.

After church, I had to explain to numerous people how Daniela was doing, and I found it depressing. I dreaded going to church. I knew they were concerned, but repeating the story over and over only made me sad. I wished they would stop asking, but their silence would have felt strange, too.

Only the closest of friends asked me how *I* was doing. Our lives revolved around Daniela's health and caring for Alex. We rarely had a chance to look after ourselves.

It was interesting how some members spoke with confidence, certain that she would recover. Others looked sad and said, "Let's hope she gets better," their tone betraying doubt.

We stayed for lunch at church and didn't get home until 4:00 p.m. Exhausted, I lay on the balcony for half an hour while Alex played.

I went to the hospital to eat dinner with Joseph. He drove to the church building to practice. I stayed with Daniela and the night nurse until 12:30 a.m., watching *Heaven Can Wait* starring Warren Beatty. I had already seen it twice and liked it every time.

Joseph picked me up so I wouldn't have to ride the bike home alone at night. That was very thoughtful of him.

BMT – Day 31

I liked Mondays. Not much happened at the hospital over the weekend, but on Mondays, both the physical therapist and the psychologist visited. On Tuesdays, Professor Dr. Feier made his weekly rounds.

Daniela had less puffiness in her eyes than two days before, but Dr. Fischer, who hadn't seen her in five days, noticed increased edema.

At 2:00 p.m., Sister Bachmann brought Alex to the hospital for a band performance in the large auditorium. We had a great time. The band played jazz as well as children's songs like "Old McDonald" and "Glory, Glory Hallelujah," closing with encores of "Summertime" and "Misty," two of my favorite songs.

We took Alex to the construction site near the *Elternhaus* since he loved watching bulldozers at work.

I returned to Daniela's room just in time to see a nurse perform another EEG, but Daniela moved her head so much that the results were useless.

Chapter 21

Family Visit from the US

Having my mother and two sisters visit me in Freiburg was a welcome change. They arrived on the same weekend as Freiburg's 875th birthday celebration. The city was buzzing with festivities, including a parade showcasing traditional local costumes. We had the opportunity to hear Joseph perform in an open-air concert with the Philharmonic Orchestra of Freiburg at the cathedral. Thousands of people gathered. It was a beautiful experience.

We crossed the border into France to visit the historic *Haut-Koenigsburg* castle in Alsace. We also visited one of my favorite little French towns, Riquewihr. The town is nestled between two city walls, its entrance framed by charming stone arches. We strolled down the cobbled street past restaurants and winemaker shops, where we could taste French wine and cheese. It was my mother's first trip to Europe, and she liked it very much. She and Olivia enjoyed the wine tasting, and each of them bought four bottles of wine to bring home in their suitcases.

I wished their visit had lasted longer than a week, but it did me good. Spending time with them eased my homesickness and provided a brief escape from the grief and anguish we had been enduring.

BMT – Day 41 (Thurs., July 6, 1995)

Daniela seemed a little bit better, her presence a little closer. Her eyes were open more often, and at times, it looked as if she fixed her gaze—if only for a second.

She also reacted to pain and stimuli more than she had in the past two weeks, though the daily changes in her consciousness were too subtle to notice.

On the other hand, I couldn't ignore the fact that Daniela's fingernails had begun to fall off. They were loose, peeling away at the base. One was entirely gone. I gently removed three others that were barely hanging on.

Dr. Zimmermann explained, "Daniela has developed an autoimmune defect. She is producing antibodies that are attacking the surface of her red blood cells."

"What does that mean?" I asked.

"It means we want to hold off on blood transfusions, since they could trigger her body to produce even more antibodies. Her hemoglobin is down to 5.6, but for now, it seems stable."

Her weight had dropped to 34 pounds (15.4 kg) from the 39.7 pounds (18 kg) she had upon admission to the hospital. Nearly three years had passed—years of growth, yet marred by weight loss due to therapy and complications. She looked painfully thin. Her calves were tiny, and each time I rubbed cream into her legs, I shuddered at how scrawny they had become.

BMT – Day 42

Dr. Fischer ordered a chest X-ray because she didn't like the way Daniela's chest sounded. She suggested that Daniela might have pneumonia. Dr. Zimmermann said they didn't yet know whether the infection was bacterial, viral, or fungal. Her CRP was between 3 and 4, verifying an infection. She had a fever of 101.8°F (38.8°C) during the night. They began treatment without knowing the exact cause, waiting for test results to confirm whether it was viral or fungal.

Joseph and I stood out in the hallway with Dr. Zimmermann and Dr. Fischer, discussing what I had brought up in a previous conversation with Dr. Zimmermann.

"If Daniela's condition worsens," Dr. Zimmermann said carefully, "it wouldn't make much sense to reanimate her or put her on a ventilator if it should come to that. It's something to think about."

Joseph agreed with Dr. Zimmermann but remained optimistic.

"She'll get through this, too," he said.

I also didn't feel affected by Dr. Zimmermann's information. Although it was good to talk about what we would or would not do if Daniela were to become critically ill again, I felt like it wouldn't come to that.

I called my mom to inform her about Daniela's two acute problems. She didn't have much to say.

"We have to hope for the best but be prepared for the worst."

"Now wait a minute," I said. "What happened to your positive thinking?"

"It's just that that poor child has been through so much."

My mother said she had trouble visualizing Daniela because she was so close to her. She could only envision surrounding Daniela with white light.

BMT – Day 43

On Day 43 Daniela began coughing up blood. Joseph and I both visualized cleaning out her lungs. '*Restore your lungs to a perfect and healthy condition*' became my mantra.

Angelina worked on Daniela from her home. Through meditation and visualization, we managed to lower Daniela's oxygen requirement from 8 to 6 liters while improving her oxygen saturation from 80% to 97%. Daniela's hemoglobin had dropped to 4.5, so she needed a blood transfusion despite the risks of aggravating her autoimmune defect.

After grocery shopping, I went to be with Daniela for three hours. That afternoon, the inauguration party for the new *Elternhaus* took place outdoors. Although it had already been in use, this was its official opening ceremony. Joseph, Alex, and Sister Bachmann joined me.

At the party, I saw Dr. Zimmermann talking with another doctor. As I started to walk past her, she held out a hand to stop me from walking by. She ended her conversation with the other person, then turned to me with a serious expression on her face. I gave her a side hug and said to her in English, "Don't make such a sad face!"

"It looks pretty bad. There's not much else we can do," she told me.

Despite the worsening X-ray, Joseph and I remained confident that Daniela would recover.

Angelina told us, "I don't see this as being serious," which confirmed my feelings and Joseph's.

Dr. Zimmermann told me, "I already told you once that we have a dying child. I feel like we're at that point again."

"Joseph and I feel that she'll get through this, too. And our healer said the same thing today."

Dr. Zimmermann may have thought that we were in denial.

After the festivities, a babysitter picked up Alex to take him home, and Joseph and I spent the evening with Daniela. Except for that serious conversation with Dr. Zimmermann, I don't remember any details about the party.

Letter to a Friend (Thurs., July 13, 1995)

In 1997, my mother encouraged me to get the Internet and an email address, but in 1995, I was still typing handwritten letters into my computer, printing them out, and sending them by mail. Delivery between Germany and the United States took about a week. At that time, a German girlfriend of mine was in the U.S. for a few months, so I wrote her the following letter:

July 13, 1995

I was so happy to receive your letter.

Your sympathy touched me deeply. I honestly don't know what you could do for me, but thank you for offering.

So far, we've remained in isolation and haven't had any visitors to avoid being exposed to viruses or bacteria.

When I'm not with Daniela, I spend time with Alex so that he doesn't feel left out. Joseph often takes him swimming (they're both water rats), and once the three of us went to the outdoor pool together.

Lately, we aren't with Daniela twelve hours a day anymore—it depends on her condition. When she's calm and asleep, she needs us less than when she's awake and restless. She was terribly restless yesterday. After having some Valium last night, she's nice and calm today, but the doctors are concerned about where this restlessness comes from. Is she in pain? She's had pneumonia since last Friday, but against all the doctors' expectations, it's getting better. She's also been on morphine since then, but they stopped it yesterday in case it was making her uneasy. That didn't help either.

Every time I put lotion on her legs, I wince. Her weight has dropped from 40 to 34 pounds, and her thighs are thinner than her knees. She has no fat left, and her muscles have shrunk a lot. A month ago in ICU, she was so swollen with fluids she couldn't have opened her eyes if she had been awake. We really experience everything with her.

I don't want to burden you, but writing about it helps me to cope.

I'm glad you like it so much in the U.S. Don't worry—I won't be moving back anytime soon. As long as Daniela is in intensive treatment, we can't leave Germany. I expect we'll stay in Freiburg for at least three to five years.

I actually like it here, but I miss my family in the U.S. and wish I could visit them more often. For three years, Daniela's frequent hospital stays have prevented me from doing so. We had planned to visit this summer, but since her diagnosis of chronic leukemia in January, travel has been impossible.

Joseph has about six weeks off beginning July 22nd and wants to visit his family with Alex for a week. Did I tell you his father has been suffering from a brain tumor since April? The prognosis looks bad. Because of Daniela, Joseph hasn't been able to visit his father yet.

Alex starts kindergarten on September 1st. Guess what! He'll be going to the same kindergarten where Daniela also went. They promised us her spot is still waiting for her.

We've had warm weather since the end of June. Too bad we can't enjoy it together as a family. Sometimes Joseph and I treat ourselves to time with Alex and leave Daniela with the nurses.

While sitting with Daniela, I have time to write (like now) and to read. I recently finished a book about angels and really enjoyed it. Daniela certainly has many angels watching over her, and they've been working overtime!

When Dr. Zimmermann told us about Daniela's pneumonia, Joseph and I remained calm and felt confident that she would recover. We told the doctors that, too. Now that her lungs are improving, they can only marvel. We hope they'll remember not to forget the spirit regardless of all the symptoms and statistics.

Since Daniela recovered from the pneumonia, Dr. Fischer said, "We never forgot that Daniela was always a Wunderkind."

She truly is a wonder, because she could have died multiple times. We can't help but wonder why she's still with us.

Wishing you all the best and greetings to your children.

Tracey

BMT – Day 50 – Regrets (Sat., July 15, 1995)

I often had mixed feelings. Day 50 was one of those days when I regretted putting Daniela through a bone marrow transplant. She was squealing—almost screaming—arching her back, straightening and tightening her legs, and bending her arms and wrists while thrashing her head back and forth. Nothing I did could calm her.

I held her on my lap, but she kept stiffening like a board and squealing until I lost control and yelled, "Now stop it, Daniela! I don't like it when you do this!"

She didn't stop—she obviously couldn't—so I put her back in bed. The doctors ended up sedating her to prevent further weight loss, because all that exertion burned too many calories. Her weight had dropped even further to 32.2 pounds (14.6 kg), with a height of 42.12 inches (107 cm). That put her BMI at 12.8—below the 1st percentile for girls her age.

I walked over to the window, staring as preparations for the summer festival at the Children's Hospital unfolded.

Life is passing you by, Daniela.

I felt so sad that she couldn't enjoy the festivities the way Joseph had hoped. He wanted her to be awake, standing at the window, waving. But she wasn't. And I couldn't enjoy the summer festival either.

I had nothing to celebrate.

Daniela's progress had been painfully slow, and neurologically, she seemed to be getting worse. It became harder and harder to visualize her recovery, and I often cried while writing in my journal.

Yet not everything was bleak. I noticed small signs of progress. Daniela had started looking at faces. She not only turned toward me but seemed to shift her gaze—from eye to eye, then to my mouth, and back to my eyes again.

"Mama. Can you say 'Mama'?"

Her lips tightened into a slight frown. She looked sad—like she *wanted* to say it but couldn't.

"You'll be able to say it soon. It'll be all right."

Never make promises like that to your child if you don't know for sure they'll come true.

Angelina called after I had turned out the lights.

"Daniela is closer now," she said. "She is more and more in the body."

"They took her off the morphine," I told her.

"That's surprising because now she can feel pain. And she is feeling pain."

"Will being in pain make it harder for her to come back into the body?"

"Certainly, it will."

Her words unsettled me. After we hung up, I called the hospital and spoke with the night nurse. She said Daniela had been given Tavor (lorazepam) to help her relax. She was able to sleep, but when she woke up, she started squealing again.

"We think she's in pain," I told the nurse. "Would the doctor consider putting her back on morphine?"

She said she would bring it up in the morning report.

The next day, the doctors followed our request and restarted Daniela on morphine.

BMT – Day 52

When I arrived to visit Daniela, I saw Hannah, the cleaning woman, rush into the bathroom with tears in her eyes. I followed her in.

"Are you crying about Daniela?"

She nodded. As she turned away, trying to hide her face, I stepped behind her and hugged her shoulders.

"I've cried a lot, too," I said.

Hannah finished cleaning the room, blinking back tears in her bloodshot eyes.

Later that day, Frau Schmidt, another cleaning woman, came in.

"Did Hannah send you?" I asked.

"Why?" she replied.

"Because she was crying this morning,"

"To be honest, I don't like coming in here anymore either."

"We're slowly losing all of our cleaning women," I said with a sigh.

Frau Schmidt walked over to Daniela's bed, leaning in close.

"Do you remember me—Frau Schmidt? We ate French fries together. You don't remember me, do you? We ate French fries together. Do you still know me?"

She repeated it over and over, as if willing Daniela to respond.

"We'll do that again—eat French fries together."

Daniela squealed and arched her back. Frau Schmidt left the room with tears in her eyes and visibly shaken.

That brought tears to my eyes, too.

I went home for lunch, and as we ate, tears once again welled up in my eyes, thinking about Daniela's condition.

"Do you think Daniela will get better?" Joseph asked.

"I don't know," I said, then broke down crying.

That evening, I called Joseph at the hospital. Since Dr. Zimmermann was in the room, I spoke with her, as well.

"Daniela is slowly waking up," she said. "All children go through a restless, frightening time during this stage."

"Do you think she's in pain?" I asked.

"It's hard to say whether she's in pain or just struggling to wake up."

"That's exactly what our healer has been telling us."

"I'm afraid you'll have to put up with her noises for a while longer and be very patient," she said gently.

"I'm at the end of my rope," I admitted.

"If you need to stay away for a day, we will completely understand. It's hard on all of us, too."

But I never considered staying away. Not even for a day.

Doll shipped from the U.S. (Mon., July 17, 1995)

When Daniela and I visited my family in January, she fell in love with my old doll. My parents had given it to me when I was about six years old. It had straight blond hair with bangs, blue eyes, and a yellow dress with white polka dots. The doll was about the height of a four-year-old child. By lifting one arm, you could make one leg move forward, allowing you to walk it while holding its hand.

Olivia wanted Daniela to have the doll, so she shipped it from Georgia to Germany—a truly sweet gesture. It took nearly seven weeks to arrive in Freiburg. Unfortunately, by the time it did, Daniela wasn't ready to receive it.

Daniela was "in," as Angelina said.

Her pneumonia had vanished, much to the doctors' amazement. However, she still suffered from an autoimmune phenomenon—a defect causing her new blood to produce antibodies that attacked the surface of her red blood cells. Not good. It could either get worse or resolve on its own. In the meantime, they administered blood transfusions but let her hemoglobin drop significantly first, hoping to avoid exacerbating the situation.

By now, I was emotionally drained, barely holding on. I had been crying for days. I wanted to believe she would get better, but every time I saw her, it was painfully hard to hold on to that hope.

BMT – Day 62 – Intracranial Pressure
(Thurs., July 27, 1995)

A new CT scan revealed that Daniela had dilated ventricles and increased intracranial pressure. On July 21st, Daniela underwent another operation to implant a surgical shunt—a tube designed to drain excess fluid from her brain to her abdomen and relieve pressure. Within a few days following the surgery, she began to have fewer screaming and stretching fits.

Talking to a psychologist felt good. I admitted how useless I felt sitting with Daniela for hours, unable to ease her pain or engage with her in any meaningful way. I felt like I was killing time while I was there, and that it wasn't good for me or Daniela. Dr. Zimmermann joined in on the conversation and said that one to two hours a day were enough. Dr. Zimmermann's words helped to ease my conscience.

Joseph believed one of us should be with Daniela most of the day, and that role usually fell to me. When the orchestra went on their summer break, Joseph left right away with Alex to visit his parents. He wanted to see his father, whose health was declining from the brain tumor. Nevertheless, I resented being left alone with Daniela, with no one to relieve me from the long hospital hours.

I applied for a part-time desk job that had opened up at the *Elternhaus*. With Alex starting kindergarten in early September and Daniela's recovery seeming more like a matter of months than weeks, I wanted to secure a job before we got deeper into debt. I also needed something to occupy my mind—freelance work no longer felt feasible.

I had useful skills—I spoke fluent German as well as native American English and could type quickly. However, I lacked the vocational training often required in Germany. Still, I figured that if I applied often enough, I would eventually find something.

BMT – Day 63

On July 28, an MRI revealed that Daniela had bleeding in the brain that was fourteen days old—meaning it had occurred before the CT scan on July 18, which hadn't detected anything. Fortunately, the pressure in her brain was gradually decreasing.

"It doesn't look like she had a hypoxemic episode," the doctor said, reassuring us that Daniela hadn't suffered oxygen deprivation that could have caused brain damage.

They replaced Daniela's special air mattress with a regular one and discontinued her morphine. I took that as a good sign.

BMT – Day 65

After I left Daniela at 9:30 p.m., I saw Aaron's father in the hallway with three other people.

"How's Daniela doing?" he asked.

"There's not much change. She still can't eat, drink or sit up, but she's starting to look directly into my eyes."

As I spoke, a woman in the group sniffled, tears welling in her eyes. I wondered why she was crying about Daniela.

Then I asked, "How is Aaron? No changes?"

Aaron's father's voice was quiet. "Aaron died today."

"Oh, I am so sorry," I said, suddenly realizing the weight of the moment. Embarrassed that I hadn't recognized the situation sooner, I gave him a hug.

"Were you expecting it?"

"Not really," he admitted. "But he had a high fever on and off for a couple of days. A few days ago, there were signs of the tumor in his urine. We knew then that it had spread through his whole body."

"He's much better off now," I said softly, searching for comforting words.

He gave a slight nod.

It had been exactly six months since the doctor told Aaron's parents that he had only hours or days to live. Yet, it had taken that long for the neuroblastoma, with metastases in his brain, to take his life.

As I rode my bike home, sadness settled over me. Aaron and Daniela had been diagnosed around the same time. They had gone through chemotherapy and radiation therapy together. Daniela had helped Aaron overcome his fear of radiation treatment. They had both relapsed in January. He had turned four in May.

Now, Aaron was dead.

BMT – Day 70 (Fri., Aug. 4, 1995)

On Day 70 following Daniela's bone marrow transplant, her hemoglobin went up a little bit on its own, but according to lab tests she was still having hemolysis; that is, she was still building antibodies that were attacking the surface of the red blood cells. Otherwise, her bilirubin was normal with a level of 1. Her liver count was still up. Her kidneys were fine. Her bowel movements were fairly normal, yet soft like the stools of a little baby that hasn't eaten solid foods yet, since she was on the tube feeding.

During an eye examination, the ophthalmologist was pleased to see that the pressure in Daniela's eyes was much better, almost normal. Things were looking up, and I felt more optimistic about Daniela's progress.

Joseph was still visiting his family in Bavaria. He kept extending his stay. He was helping his family sort and throw out twenty years' worth of junk that had piled up—things that his father had collected. He helped paint some rooms, too. He said that Alex was having a great time. They had their own yard complete with a sandbox. Alex was so engrossed in playing that he only wanted to talk on the phone with me once.

I told Joseph the exciting news that Daniela was noticeably better and that she was no longer screaming for hours like she used to.

I had stayed with her for six hours, and she was relaxed the entire time. While she used to get upset and start straightening her legs and stiffening up, within a few days after the shunt was implanted, I was able to immediately calm her down just by adjusting her position in the stroller or in bed. I rejoiced that first day when she didn't get stiff all day long. That alone was an amazing improvement compared to the previous two weeks when she would stiffen up like a board, and you couldn't bend her until she relaxed again.

I joked that she could appear in a magic show. We could have placed one chair under her head and another under her feet, and they would have held her up. I would say anything to make a serious situation feel less burdensome.

At this point, I had the mornings and evenings to myself and spent the afternoons with Daniela. Since she was more awake, and I was able to calm her down, I felt better about being with her. She seemed to be looking at me intensely, as if she recognized me. That was the first time I felt this since she returned from intensive care seven weeks earlier.

Her eye contact was much better. She no longer turned her head constantly from side to side as she had before. She made only slight movements but maintained eye contact. She no longer held her hands in fists, and her arms were much more relaxed.

The doctors took her off the Atosil (promethazine), which they had given her day and night to calm her down. They began to unhook all of Daniela's IVs each afternoon, so that I could take her outside in the stroller for thirty minutes. When she sat in the stroller, she almost rested her left arm on her lap—though she still held her right wrist bent and flailed it about, unable to control it. Once she was situated, I would push her up and down the hallway of the *Pfaundler* wing for another half hour or until I was called back into the room to hook everything up again.

Every afternoon I fed Daniela through her nasogastric or NG tube, which is a thin, flexible plastic tube that is inserted through the nose, down the esophagus, and into the stomach. Since Daniela couldn't eat, she was fed special nutrition through this tube. It was also used to administer oral medication. At night, she received an injection of lorazepam to help her relax and sleep.

I had an interview with a temporary work agency. The man who interviewed me felt that I was overqualified for an office position. He was afraid that I wouldn't be satisfied with it. He was considering me for another position within the agency that would be more challenging. (I don't remember now what kind of position it was.)

He sent me home to think about it, which was a good idea. I definitely wasn't satisfied with the salary he would be paying for temporary office work. His agency would take a cut of my earnings, like any other temp agency, so I figured I'd be better off finding a permanent position. The only problem was that most German employers want to see some kind of proof of training. Experience or the ability to learn quickly didn't seem to count. Their idea of on-the-job training was in the form of an apprenticeship, which paid very little.

I hadn't heard from the *Elternhaus* since I interviewed there three weeks earlier. They wanted to hire someone by August 1, which had come and gone, so I figured they must have taken someone else.

Chapter 22

Family Matters

Olivia sent me a fax to let me know that Nana's health was declining. Lynn had found our grandmother lying face down on the bedroom floor, estimated she had been there for about twenty hours, and immediately called an ambulance. Although Nana had no broken bones, a CT scan revealed multiple infarcts in her brain, leading to a diagnosis of dementia. These infarcts were the result of transient ischemic attacks (TIAs), which are often precursors to strokes. While the TIAs weren't new, the visible infarcts on the scan were.

Nana had moments of deep confusion—sometimes unable to recall what she'd had for lunch—while at other times, she was bitterly convinced that family members or others had stolen from her or were scheming to put her in a nursing home just to take her belongings.

She was eighty-four and had become unable to live by herself. Poor Lynn was bombarded with non-stop phone calls with Nana repeating the same orders and demands over and over.

There were plenty more details, but I didn't feel the need to call my mother and hear them. I thought that would be too much for me at the time, since Joseph and I were so surrounded by sickness and hospitals with Daniela and Joseph's father.

Joseph took Alex with him to visit his family in Bavaria for about three weeks. He was almost ready to come home, so I took a train to meet them. I spent only a couple of days there, and the three of us drove back to Freiburg together.

When I first saw Joseph's father lying in bed asleep looking so helpless, I had to fight back the tears. He was able to answer questions with yes and no or with short sentences, but only in a whisper. He was confined to a bed or a wheelchair and could feed himself pieces of bread, but otherwise he had to be fed his soup or given something to drink. He was no longer crawling around on the floor like he used to, so it had become easier on Joseph's mother.

After we returned to Freiburg, Joseph's father suffered another epileptic attack and was hospitalized again. His body stiffened, and he clenched his teeth. He couldn't get any air. Joseph went back to Bavaria again at the end of August and left Alex with me.

I had a sore throat for over two weeks that had developed into a little bit of a cough, so I stayed away from Daniela or visited her outside of her hospital room until Joseph left for Bavaria. Alex had a slightly runny nose, so he wore a mask when he visited her in the hospital. Whenever we went outside with Daniela in a stroller, Daniela had to wear a face mask.

I still had some help from Sister Bachmann from Monday evening to Friday evening. She slept in my office and went to bed early, so I couldn't spend time at the computer like I wanted to. The rule was that a missionary served in one home but slept in another. We were looking for a family from church for her to stay with so that she wouldn't have to be with us all the time. I needed her household help, but it was difficult having her there 24/7.

Sometimes I preferred having peace and quiet. With everything going on—Joseph's father's decline, Daniela's fragile stage, the stress I had to endure, and the constant presence of Sister Bachmann—I felt like I was being stretched too thin. Even small things, like her overly animated tone, started to wear on me. Even Joseph said he was beginning to dislike the Swiss accent, especially the kind where the voice rises and falls as if they were singing while speaking.

I could finally appreciate what Joseph meant when he came home from work or from the hospital and said that he needed a few minutes to unwind before being bombarded with questions or stories from me or Alex. I felt the same way when I came home from the hospital, and Sister Bachmann pumped my ears full.

"Alex is fine when he is with me," she said. "But when you or your husband are around, Alex won't let me do anything."

"He wants us to put his clothes on him when we're here," I said.

"It's frustrating for me. Normally children always like me. I don't understand why I'm having trouble with Alex."

"I guess you've never worked with a child who had a sibling in the hospital," I said, trying to alleviate her distress. Although, I suspected that Alex was picking up on our discomfort with the whole situation when we were around Sister Bachmann. Children can be very perceptive.

Daniela was still showing small but steady amounts of progress. Her eye contact had gotten much better, and she even turned her head to look at the source of a sound. A few weeks earlier, Daniela also started to laugh. At first, she laughed at something I did, but when I repeated it later, she didn't laugh, making it seem like random laughter. But soon she definitely seemed to laugh at things that she thought were funny. We began playing children's videos again in her room. While she was watching *Snow White*, she laughed whenever the dwarves appeared—especially during scenes where Grumpy was being washed and had his teeth brushed, or when Sneezy sneezed and blew everyone across the room. It was wonderful for us to hear her laugh. She almost sounded like the old Daniela.

She wasn't making any progress with her intake of nutrition, though. She was still unable to swallow. We kept trying to give her a bottle or a glass of something to drink or a spoonful of baby applesauce, but she pressed her lips together. When she did have something in her mouth, it dribbled right back out, or she pushed it out with her tongue. She was drooling a lot, too.

So, while she was being fed through her NG tube, she kept vomiting almost every day. The doctors changed the amount or concentration of nutrition that they gave her, but it didn't help. She was still getting a TPN, a total parenteral nutrition through the IV as the major source of nutrition, since she still had an impairment of her gastrointestinal function. She had some congestion in her upper lungs too, and for three weeks her coughing hadn't gone away.

Mallorca with Alex

I decided it was time for a break. On September 6, Alex and I took a one-week vacation with a friend of mine and her daughter, Tanja, who was Daniela's age. We flew from Basel, Switzerland, to Mallorca, an island off the coast of Spain (near Ibiza, where we had vacationed as a family the previous summer.) Freiburg had already turned chilly—about 50°F (10°C) during the day—so we were hoping for a little more sunshine. More than anything, I just needed to get away.

Job Search and Choir Blues

I had been applying for jobs for four weeks, facing one rejection after another. I longed for a steady job that would get me out of the house, somewhere I had to be at 8 o'clock in the morning. Working from home had proven too difficult—I couldn't discipline myself with so many distractions around.

I called up the president of the pop choir that I had been conducting before Daniela's bone marrow transplant. While I had taken a break to be with Daniela, they had hired a substitute to fill in for me. I let the president know that I would be returning for the new season in September.

She told me there were mixed feelings among the choir members—some were so pleased with the substitute conductor that they wanted to keep him, while others insisted, "That's not fair to Tracey." Sixteen singers voted to keep the substitute, while nine voted to have me come back. I was devastated and had to stifle my tears during the phone call.

According to my contract, they were required to give me three months' notice. I knew I could prove my worth in that time. I told the president she can bet on me working harder than ever to convince the choir to keep me. But she informed me they would simply pay me upfront for the next three months. That meant I wouldn't even have the chance to rehearse with them or prove myself—they didn't want me back.

I guess I couldn't blame them. I had been too open during rehearsals, often sharing updates about Daniela. I should have kept that to myself.

I cried after that phone call. The next day, when the official notice arrived, tears welled up again. I had earned a *Master of Music, magna cum laude,* yet I no longer had anything to show for it. I felt completely rejected.

Months later, a choir member told me that about a third of the singers quit in protest after the board refused to let me return. That felt bittersweet.

Bouts of Depression

Nana passed away in September 1995, about four weeks after Lynn found her on the floor. With Daniela in the hospital and Joseph at work, I didn't fly over for her memorial. I hoped my family in the U.S. understood.

During this time, I felt depressed and was often close to tears. Joseph and I were fighting a lot, too. We disagreed about whether I should work. I had taken on a few piano students again but wanted to find a steady job. He wanted me to stay home with the children. I didn't mean to insult him, but I pointed out that his income alone wasn't enough to cover our expenses.

We trimmed down our expenses as much as we could, including selling our new car for an older model. I suppose we could have sold it altogether, since it was a major monthly expense, but I wasn't willing to go without one. I prefer doing one big grocery run per week by car rather than biking to the market every day with a backpack. Not to mention, having a car is nice for trips outside the city.

I also needed some kind of activity or distraction. I felt like I was going stir-crazy. Joseph still didn't seem to understand that. But even he admitted to feeling antsy after spending entire days at the hospital.

I felt that we needed counseling. The stress we were under was enormous, so it was no surprise that neither of us could lift the other up. Joseph was away from Daniela, but, with his father's illness, there was no escaping sickness and suffering.

Joseph and I did a project together. We decided to paint our bedroom, which meant we had to move all the furniture away from the walls. Since the closets were freestanding and not built-in, we had to empty them in order to move them. We painted the room a pale green and ordered new sheets and curtains. We moved our furniture around, so the bed was by the window, and the closets were on the opposite side of the room. It looked really good. Joseph was uneasy about sleeping under an open window. He was afraid that a draft might make him sick.

I told him that in the wintertime we have the windows closed, and most of the spring and summer we have to close them because of our allergies. Before Joseph left to visit his family in Bavaria, he painted the kids' room a deep shade of blue. It ended up being a lot darker than I wanted, but it still looked pretty good. I hung up new curtains with *The Lion King* motif and made the beds with matching bedspreads. By then, Alex had outgrown his crib. When he returned from visiting Oma and saw his new bedroom, a smile spread across his face as he ran to his bed and jumped into it.

During this time, I felt that Daniela's recovery was much too slow. The doctors said that we needed to have a lot of patience. I wondered if part of my depression stemmed from mourning for the old Daniela. I missed her, and I wanted her back.

When friends asked how Alex was doing, I wasn't sure how to answer. I think he was suffering, too. He seemed to need a lot of hugging and kissing, and he gave me a lot of hugs and kisses. If I raised my voice at him over something, he would frown and say, "Don't be so mean!"

Other Sick Children

New children or children with relapses were constantly coming into the oncology wing. It was frightening and saddening to witness. A girl returned to the hospital who we knew during Daniela's first illness. She also had neuroblastoma three years earlier in her adrenal gland. She had returned with metastases in her brain. The doctors wanted to try a stem cell transplant, which has been performed on adults for CML (chronic myeloid leukemia), but this would be the first time it would be done on a child in Freiburg.

Yet another child, a three-year-old who had CMML since birth, was readmitted to the hospital with 60,000 white blood cells. The previous fall, she had undergone a bone marrow transplant in Munich. The biopsy performed in Freiburg confirmed a recurrence of her CMML.

I spoke to Dr. Zimmermann about that.

"It really scares me to hear about this little girl's relapse."

"I understand," she said. "But I've put the possibility of a recurrence for Daniela out of my mind."

"Really? Why?" I asked.

"Because she has such a strong Graft vs. Host Disease. That significantly reduces the risk of the leukemia coming back."

"I didn't realize that."

Dr. Zimmermann nodded. "In contrast, the three-year-old barely reacted to the new bone marrow."

Amid all the worrying news, we finally had some good news about Daniela. She was making good blood. Her hemoglobin continued to climb, and her platelets were rising. She hadn't needed a blood transfusion for several weeks. Her white blood cells were being kept at bay with the cyclosporine and cortisone, which were also causing some side effects. Her eyebrows had grown dark and bushy from the cyclosporine, and her cheeks had become round and puffy from the cortisone. The doctors told us that some children develop a hairy back, so we were glad that Daniela only had Brooke Shields's eyebrows along with hamster cheeks. They said that once she was taken off the medicine six months later, all those side effects would go away.

I had a dream about Daniela. I heard her speak her first two words since her cardiac arrest—her voice was soft but clear, like music to my ears. Then she talked more and more. I was so happy in my dream that I wanted to tell everyone Daniela was talking again.

In another dream about Daniela, we were with Mommy and Daddy and most of the family. Daniela was there and was talking, and we were all getting ready to sit down for dinner.

I asked in amazement, "Can she sit up by herself?"

And she could! She was better in my dream. I had maybe two other dreams like that following her bone marrow transplant. In both, Daniela and I were together, and I suddenly realized she was completely well. I was overjoyed.

How I wished those dreams would come true!

Letter to Family (Fri., Sept. 29, 1995)

Today Joseph and I had a 30-minute meeting with Dr. Fischer, a nurse, the psychologist, and the physical therapist to discuss Daniela's progress. They explained that when Daniela is awake, she wants attention, but they're not able to give it to her all day long. They said it would be good if I could be at the hospital at 11:30 a.m.

Joseph stepped in to say that he is at work, Alex needs to be picked up from kindergarten at noon, and I need to prepare lunch. He said how important this family time is for us. He asked them if it would be possible to take Daniela off the IVs earlier in the day. (Right now, she gets unhooked after the afternoon report, around 2:30 p.m.) Dr. Fischer said it might be possible to run her cyclosporine more quickly—in two hours instead of four—and unhook her by 11:30. After our meeting, she talked with Dr. Zimmermann and let us know that we will be able to take Daniela home at 11:30! We just have to bring her back around 6:30 p.m.

A nurse said that I would have to give Daniela her medicine through the NG tube once at home in the afternoon. She has clostridium again and has to take Clont (metronidazole). Two days ago, I was unhappy to hear that Daniela has clostridium and that the medicine she needs to take can only be given "per os," which means they had to reinsert an NG tube since she still couldn't swallow. Since then, they've been giving her the Clont mashed up and mixed with Oralpädon, which is a clear electrolyte mix normally given to replace fluids when you have diarrhea. She has diarrhea from the clostridium.

Joseph made a statement during our meeting this morning that "we already feel guilty that Daniela is alone all night." I said to him, "Do you feel guilty? She sleeps the entire time!" I wonder if he was exaggerating or if there was some truth to his statement. I think he meant to say that we feel guilty that we don't spend our mornings in the clinic.

I've decided <u>not</u> to feel guilty, because I know that if I spend too many hours in the clinic, I get exhausted and irritable, and our family life suffers. I have to set a limit in order to pace myself for the months ahead. Daniela is at Day 120 since the bone marrow transplant, and she's been in the hospital almost five months now. There was a time when I fled to the hospital to avoid responsibilities at home. Then I escaped the pressures of the hospital by going home. All I wanted to do was escape. Now I try to enjoy where I am and not feel guilty that I'm not somewhere else. That feeling continually creeps in, but I try to ignore it and not dwell on it.

Shortly after the transplant in early June, a rash developed all over Daniela's body. The doctors weren't sure if it was a reaction to the chemotherapy, the morphine she needed at the time, or the new bone marrow. While Daniela was in the ICU, she developed blisters all along the edges of her ears, and her skin turned dark over the course of a few days. The bone marrow affects all the organs, and the skin is the largest organ. Since then, it has gotten paler, but anyone who sees her now still asks why she is so dark.

Tonight, I was talking to the mother of another child who has acute lymphatic leukemia (ALL). She asked me why Daniela's skin was so dark. When I explained that Daniela had undergone a bone marrow transplant and that her darker skin was a result of Graft vs. Host Disease, the woman asked if the bone marrow donor had been a black person! I couldn't help but laugh. It was a rather logical assumption for someone unfamiliar with the condition, yet, at the same time, completely illogical!

But here's some interesting information. While Daniela was in the ICU, Dr. Zimmermann told me that they were going to check Daniela's blood for a male marker. Apparently, there are markers in the blood that indicate whether the blood comes from a male or a female. I was surprised to hear that.

"Does that have any consequences? I asked.

"If you mean, will she grow a beard? No. It has no effect on her."

Later, Dr. Zimmermann told us, "Daniela's blood has a male marker, so that means it is Alex's blood. That's good news."

By the end of the week, Sister Bachmann gets on my nerves. It's Friday night, midnight, and I'm able to write in my journal, which I write on my computer. Sister Bachmann sleeps in our office, so I feel I'm intruding when I do office work. When I came home tonight, I was in a much better mood since she had gone home for the weekend. Starting next week, she will be sleeping at Jakob's home, so maybe I'll feel less stressed.

This afternoon, we took Daniela with us to buy groceries. It was a good thing Sister Bachmann came along. The shopping carts didn't have a place for a child to sit, so I pushed a cart with the food while she pushed the cart with the kids sitting on a blanket that I had pulled from the car. At one point, Daniela was crying, and we didn't know what was wrong. Two shoppers stood nearby, and one of the women stared a hole through Daniela. I felt like saying something but decided not to be as rude as she was being. Daniela had an NG tube taped to her face and had pulled off her cap, so you could see the bump on her head where the shunt is. Plus, her hair is really short. I suppose I would stare, too.

By the way, when I returned with Alex from Mallorca on September 13, I noticed that Daniela's hair is growing. It's dark, too. I don't know if it will stay dark or if that's still a side effect from the cyclosporine. She still has several wisps of blond hair hanging down in the front on the right and at the nape of her neck, but the left side was shaved for the shunt surgery. Not too long ago I cut off the longer strands, since the new hair is coming in. Several people said it looks much better now.

I remember thinking how strange it looked when other children only have a few long strands of hair, but for some reason, I never thought Daniela looked odd. I even told the anesthesiologist, "Please tell the surgeon we're grateful for every hair and ask him to shave as little as possible." He did. Some children's heads were shaved completely, but this way, Daniela was never fully bald during this latest treatment. Her hair is still very short and thin, so it doesn't look healthy yet, but it should look better soon.

Daniela enjoys walking with our help. She's getting stronger every day. We still have to hold her hands, but she's placing more of her weight on her legs and not on her arms. Now she can support her weight when she is standing, but she still needs our help for balance. She still doesn't stretch her arms out much, so today I put on some music and practiced "conducting" with her, waving her arms to the beat. Sometimes she loosened up for a few bars of the music.

She often moves both arms up and wraps them around her head as if she's trying to hide. This movement is often uncontrolled, but she does it whenever someone wants to do something to her face or when she's tired. When someone leaves and waves "bye bye," Daniela tries to wave, but instead, she brings both arms up in front of her with her right palm open, and then they move up to hide her head again.

The psychologist thinks Daniela is trying to speak. She thought she heard Daniela making "na" or "nye" sounds for "no" or "nein," and that she may have been trying to say "Mama." I haven't heard that yet, although I've been repeating it to Daniela over and over with the hopes that she'll imitate me. The psychologist also said that Daniela's feelings have become more differentiated. Daniela used to smile at anyone that came in the room and cry at anyone who left. Now, she looks to see who comes into the room and doesn't smile at everyone. She no longer cries when anyone else leaves, but she does cry when Mama or Papa goes.

Next Wednesday, the doctors plan to insert a PEG tube, which means another surgery for Daniela. The tube will go through her belly into her stomach and down into the first part of the duodenum. Since she hasn't been able to keep food down, they placed a tube through her nose all the way down into her duodenum on September 18 under general anesthesia by way of an endoscopy, which uses a tube with a light and a special camera at the end. The procedure showed that her esophagus was inflamed, but there seems to be no mechanical reason why Daniela is vomiting.

The next morning, Daniela pulled the tube out. They've tried to insert a few more tubes since then while Daniela was awake, and it was torture for everyone involved. I asked one of the nurses, "Is this stressful for you, too?" He sighed and replied, "Can't you tell?"

In fact, last Thursday, September 21, Joseph was with Daniela when they tried to put a tube in. He was so upset by the procedure and her screaming that when he got home from work, he said, "I'm too tired to go to the wedding reception tonight. I'm not in the mood, either." (We'd been invited by a newlywed couple from church.)

I felt really disappointed, because I was going to sing two Barbra Streisand songs and wanted him to hear me. It was my debut singing pop music with a microphone. I told him, "You just need to change your mood." He said something about having the freedom of choice, and he chooses to stay home. It brought tears to my eyes and dampened my mood for the rest of the evening.

Oh, dear. This letter has gotten to be long again. Joseph has been asleep for 2-1/2 hours already, and Alex is going to wake me up in the morning. Now is a good time to close.

Love you, Tracey

Chapter 23

The Story of Annemarie

We half-heartedly tried to restart our network marketing business. In March, I had qualified for the company's Leader's Club. Even though I hadn't been able to do much business since then, the company was covering travel expenses for all Leaders' Club members to attend the conference in Memphis. I had never been to Memphis before, and they were paying for my airfare. I planned to fly from Frankfurt to Memphis, stay in a hotel, and fly back.

For some unknown reason, I felt compelled to call my friend, Annemarie, to see if she could meet me in Memphis. Annemarie was one of only two friends I had stayed in touch with since high school. She was three years younger than me. We both played in the high school band and bonded instantly. We had sleepovers at each other's houses, and I would go with her to the Baptist church whenever she sang a solo. She had such a naturally beautiful singing voice. In fact, I had named Daniela's middle name, Marie, after her.

I called her in early September, and she agreed to meet me in Memphis.

A few weeks later, before I had booked my flight, I called her back.

"Hello?" came a sleepy voice.

"Hey, Annemarie, this is Tracey."

"Hi."

She didn't sound very enthusiastic.

"Did you book a flight to Memphis?" I asked.

"Memphis?" she said blankly.

"In October. I wanted to meet you in Memphis."

"No. I forgot."

"Are you all right?" Something about her voice sounded off.

"Yeah, I'm just tired," she mumbled.

Her speech was slurred. Had she been drinking? Or was she on drugs? That wasn't like her at all.

"Never mind," I said. "I'm coming there."

I decided on the spot that I needed to see her in person. If she was struggling with drinking—or anything else—I wanted to be there for her.

I booked a flight to Memphis, then another from Memphis to Atlanta, and a return flight to Frankfurt.

The convention was uplifting, designed to fire us up for our network marketing business. Fellow networkers shared their success stories, and I felt motivated.

But any inspiration I gained was completely forgotten by the days that followed.

When I arrived in Atlanta, I rented a car and drove two hours north to Blairsville. I had barely stepped into my mom's house when the phone rang. It was Lucy, my other close high school friend. The three of us—Lucy, Annemarie, and I—had been inseparable. Lucy had even lived with Annemarie's family for a while.

"Annemarie is dying," she blurted. Lucy had never been one to soften bad news.

"What do you mean—dying?" I asked, my heart pounding.

"She's in the hospital. Can you come down to Gainesville?"

After Lucy's sketchy information, I got the full report from my sister, Lynn, who lived in Gainesville, and had worked as a registered nurse with Annemarie's mother in public health. She filled in the missing pieces.

It had started with a minor car accident—a fender bender at low speed. Afterward, Annemarie began having trouble with memory and word recall. When she developed blurred vision and numbness in her hand, the doctors ordered an MRI. The results were devastating. Annemarie had a malignant brain tumor.

During surgery to remove the tumor, she hemorrhaged into the brain stem. They inserted a shunt to drain the blood, but it clogged up, and she went back into surgery. Now she was in the ICU, unresponsive, on life support, with no brain activity.

I couldn't believe it.

Without hesitation, I drove straight back to Gainesville and met Lucy at the hospital.

When I entered the room and saw Annemarie lying on the bed in the ICU with all the tubes and the ventilator going, it seemed surreal. I thought of Daniela. I was so used to seeing my small daughter lying in bed that it struck me that Annemarie looked so big—so long—lying there in the bed, even though she had a petite stature.

Lucy and I each said a prayer out loud. We were saying our goodbyes.

"Annemarie," I prayed, "if anything should happen to Daniela, please take care of her."

I immediately wondered why I would say that. There was no need for Annemarie to take care of Daniela because Daniela was getting better. *Wasn't she?*

Two days later, on October 16, 1995, Annemarie's parents agreed to turn off the life support machines. During that one week in Georgia, I saw my girlfriend for the last time and attended her funeral. I was astonished at the synchronicity.

I was a mess at the funeral. Tears streamed down my cheeks. I was heartbroken that my dear friend had died. Annemarie, Lucy, and I had performed together in the high school band. Annemarie was one month shy of her thirty-third birthday when she passed away. She left her husband and a ten-year-old son behind. Her beautiful singing voice was silenced much too early.

At the funeral, I had only one comforting thought: *You made it.*

Through my deep sorrow, I almost envied her. Annemarie no longer had to suffer or deal with problems in life. I had no idea what lay ahead for me. Somehow, I longed to be released from all my problems, but I had two small children who needed me.

Letter to Family (Sun., Nov. 12, 1995)

Joseph's father has been progressively getting worse from his brain tumor since April. Joseph and his brothers and sisters don't get along with their father. Joseph fortunately had a good talk with his dad this summer, forgiving him and expressing his love. He also encouraged his brothers and sisters to do the same, but they're not willing. Joseph was the oldest and left home at the age of 17, so he missed the worst years of his father's tyranny. He always caught a taste of it whenever he went home to visit.

We had a talk with Dr. Zimmermann this week. We brought up the subject of a rehab center, but Dr. Zimmermann said that as long as Daniela has an IV and is being fed through the stomach tube, a rehab center will not take her. They may not even take her if she's only on the stomach tube. Dr. Zimmermann and the psychologist and physical therapist all think that it would be better for Daniela to be at home and not to be sent off someplace else. They're working out a plan to have two different kinds of physical therapists come to our home to work with Daniela.

I told them that I didn't think she was getting enough therapy. The psychologist said, "You probably think that if we do more, she'll show more progress," and I said, "Yes, I do." However, they explained that Daniela often falls asleep during the therapy sessions, and more therapy would be too much for her.

The current goal is to increase the nutrition she is getting through the stomach tube and get her off total parenteral nutrition. Until then, she won't be able to go home. They're guessing it could take 4 to 6 weeks, but they've been saying that for the past two or three weeks. Daniela is receiving Pregomin through the stomach tube, a formula even less complex than what is given to babies with milk allergies. Yet, she's still having trouble absorbing it. Her bowels were undoubtedly messed up from the Graft vs. Host Disease, and it's going to take a long time for them to recover.

Daniela keeps coming up with clostridium in her stools, and her liver count keeps going way up and then back down again. They're saying that the clostridium may be in the gallbladder passages and affecting the liver. She's going to be on Clont for a longer period of time to get it under control.

Joseph drove to Bavaria today to visit with his family for three days, especially to see his father. Now I have a chance to hold down the fort by myself. Joseph did a good job while I was in the U.S., except I returned home to a week's worth of laundry.

More news later.

Lots of hugs and love, Tracey

Death in the Family

Joseph's father died on Thursday morning, November 16, 1995. Joseph was already in Bavaria. Alex and I took a train on Sunday to be there for the funeral on Monday.

I had a quiet, uneventful birthday with my in-laws. Since it was the day after Joseph's father's funeral—and it was freezing outside—we didn't feel like going out to celebrate.

Joseph stayed in Bavaria a few days longer than me. He had to call in sick to work—a doctor wrote him an excuse. It was a good decision, because Joseph was a big help to his mother with funeral arrangements and paperwork.

While we were away, a friend picked up Daniela from the hospital each day and brought her to our home, following our usual routine. The psychologist and physical therapist both told me how excited they were about the substantial progress that Daniela had made within one week. Her hand coordination was much better, and it was obvious that she understood language.

The psychologist looked at a book with her and asked Daniela, "Where is the man with the package? Where is the lady with the flowers?"

Daniela picked them out among several choices. She was able to express herself a little better by frowning or shaking her head "no" and smiling for yes.

The psychologist wanted to do some tests and find a speech therapist for Daniela.

On December 1, 1995, I started a job at the University Medical Center as a medical records transcriptionist—in German! I got up early and worked from 7:45 to 11:45 a.m. Even though I had put myself through college by typing medical records, I was surprised at how quickly I picked up German medical terminology.

Chapter 24

Slow Recovery at Home

Daniela had been in the hospital for seven months straight when we finally took her home in December.

We wanted to take Daniela to see Disney's *Pocahontas* at the movie theater, but she had a slight fever, so the doctors declined the idea. Dr. Zimmermann personally called me back to explain that Daniela's immune system was extremely suppressed and that she needed to avoid crowds for the next six months. What a bummer. I would have enjoyed the movie, too, but I had to wait until it came out on DVD.

After we returned from a visit to the doctor to check Daniela's CRP, which was slightly above normal and didn't require antibiotics, the four of us sat in front of the TV with a big bowl of American microwave popcorn and watched a children's video. Daniela was exhausted by the end and went straight to bed at 8:00 p.m. with Alex following soon after.

Daniela began to eat, but only little bits. She had noticeably eaten much more in the hospital, but at least she was no longer throwing up. I figured the cortisone she was receiving had increased her appetite, but that was a good side effect in this case. We were happy to see her eating. She wasn't eating enough to gain weight, though, so she was still being fed formula through her PEG tube.

A percutaneous endoscopic gastrostomy (PEG) is a procedure in which a tube is inserted through the abdomen into the stomach to provide a means of feeding when the patient cannot eat enough through the mouth. I had to mix Daniela's liquid nutrition every day, draw it up in a 50 ml syringe, and place it in the syringe pump, which slowly injected the nutrition through the PEG tube. The central venous catheter, on the other hand, was mainly used for pain medication.

Since Daniela was being fed through her PEG tube for over nineteen hours, she woke up three times a night needing a diaper change, and then she didn't go back to sleep right away. Because of this, we were getting very little sleep.

Alex had regressed lately—wetting the bed at night and having accidents during the day—which meant he needed a diaper. We had to remind him to use the toilet, as he often seemed to forget until it was too late.

We thought maybe he was somewhat jealous of all the attention that Daniela was getting. Sometimes he pushed her around, causing her to fall down. On the other hand, he played big brother and talked excitedly whenever Daniela was able to do something new.

Had Daniela let me sleep at night, I think I could have handled the daytime stress much better. The hardest part was that when Joseph went into her room at night, she kept screaming. She wanted me. While she cried with Joseph in the room, I lay awake in bed.

So much for taking turns.

Daniela was still having seizure-like activity, even though in December an EEG showed only slight abnormalities, but nothing that you could put a label on. She made sudden movements, gasping sharply as she did. If she was sitting down, she would hit her head on the table or fall out of her chair. If she was standing up or trying to walk, she would suddenly fall over backward and sometimes hit her head on the floor.

Over the course of several weeks, Daniela slowly regained her walking ability without falling over, but she was still unsure on her feet. She could move from standing to sitting on the floor, but she couldn't stand up from the floor.

Her fine motor coordination showed a little improvement. When we played children's board games, she had difficulty throwing the dice, but she remembered how to play the games we used to play. She could no longer connect two Duplo pieces or pull them apart. She was able to set tall blocks on the floor, but she often got frustrated when they fell over.

We always hoped that Daniela would fully recover, that she would talk again and play like other children. My daughter lost her speech on June 4th when she went into cardiac arrest. It was apparent that she understood us when we spoke to her in both German and English, but she could no longer talk. She would say a long "aah" for "*ja*" or "yes" and a short "nah" for "*nein*" or "no." Not hearing her talk anymore was probably one of the saddest things for me.

Even when Daniela couldn't speak and had to be carried around at six years old, I kept waiting and hoping for her recovery. A child who was born with special needs has little or no hope of improvement. Daniela had become mentally and physically challenged, but when strangers looked at me with sympathy in their eyes, I wanted to scream out, "She's not stupid! She had cancer and things went wrong. She can't walk or talk now, but she's in there somewhere. She understands everything I say!"

I used to feel sorry for parents who had a child with a mental or physical disability. I always thought that I couldn't handle that. I suddenly had a child with disabilities, and my healthy child had been taken from me. It felt like two blows at once.

On another note, Joseph gave himself a remote-controlled car for Christmas that the kids were allowed to use. The four of us put on our coats and went out for a walk on a sunny winter day. Alex rode his bike, and we pushed Daniela in her stroller. She enjoyed watching the little car drive around. Then we put the controls in her hands. She couldn't steer the car, but she was able to make it move forward. I thought maybe this was something she could learn how to do while sitting in her stroller. At this point, Daniela was able to take short steps on her own, but she couldn't walk long distances.

Hospitalization (January 11, 1996)

During the four weeks following Christmas, neither Joseph nor I observed any seizure activity in Daniela. But in January, she developed a rash that spread across her entire body within four days. Her last night at home before being admitted to the hospital was a sleepless night. She kept me awake, whimpering and scratching and wanting anti-itch cream, which didn't help much. At 3:00 a.m. I woke Joseph up.

"Huh?" he said, half asleep.

"It's your turn. I've got to get some sleep, too."

Daniela kept Joseph awake until 6:30 a.m., when she finally fell asleep from exhaustion. When she was admitted to the hospital, we were able to get some sleep at home again.

At the hospital, the doctors suspected and confirmed that she had Graft versus Host Disease again, but that it was chronic instead of acute. During the first six months following a bone marrow transplant, GvHD is acute, but when it occurs after six months, it is considered to be chronic. A chronic GvHD can become a severe complication of a bone marrow transplant. I didn't like the sound of that.

Her liver was apparently affected, too, because her GPT was slightly raised at 160 when she entered the hospital. It went up to 500 despite the cortisone and cyclosporine that she was getting. She also tested positive again for clostridia in her stool, so the doctors weren't certain if the liver problem was related to the clostridia or to the GvHD.

I enjoyed my new job at the University Hospital. It gave me a break from constantly caring for a sick child, which I felt was important for my well-being. My contract was limited until the end of March, but I figured I would apply for another job within the *Uniklinik*. I heard that it's much easier to get another job once you're in the system.

In November, I was called to be the church choir conductor. It was a nice opportunity since I had lost my other chorus, but it was unpaid. All church callings were voluntary, yet you were "called" by the bishop or one of his counselors. You were also taught to accept all callings. Hardly anyone requested to be released from a calling.

Baby Teeth

Daniela lost her second baby tooth in February 1996. Her first tooth had fallen out after Christmas, but I never found it. We managed to save the second one, though. Her baby teeth were pushed out by the adult teeth, since she didn't move them around with her tongue to loosen them like I always did as a kid. As a result, the baby tooth stuck out at an angle until it finally fell out while she was eating. The two new teeth were on the bottom at the front.

Since her last discharge from the hospital, Daniela had begun sleeping through the night, and I was deeply grateful for that. If only I had learned to go to bed earlier… But I'm a night owl and probably always will be.

At the beginning of March 1996 Daniela came down with a fever and had pain in her belly. She had to be treated in the hospital with IV antibiotics. Her fever was still high after four days, so she was given a second antibiotic until it got better.

It could take a long time before she would be healthy enough to not have to go to the hospital every time that she got sick. If the Graft vs. Host Disease were to remain chronic, she would be sick and under a doctor's care the rest of her life. *Some life*, I thought.

I was grateful that she was alive, but I still felt so frustrated that she couldn't talk. Her health problems caused by the GvHD along with feeding her through the gastrostomy tube and her inability to eat were enough to deal with, but her lack of speech made her seem like a totally different person.

Daniela didn't seem to have any cognitive problems, though. She understood speech and could point at things in a book that I asked about. Her fine motor coordination was still lacking. She could only scribble on a page and couldn't draw or write anymore. Other children her age were already learning how to read and write. Part of learning to read involves sounding out words aloud. I wondered how a child who couldn't speak could learn to read.

Daniela underwent physical therapy twice a week, speech therapy twice a week, and ergotherapy once a week. As far as I could tell, none of them were focusing on her reading or writing. All the therapists worked with Daniela in our home. The physical therapist, who had been coming the longest, completed her twentieth session with Daniela.

The speech therapist built a rapport with Daniela first and was working on ways to help her eat. Chewing strengthens the muscles in the mouth, tongue, and jaw—essential for speech—so the reasoning was that Daniela wouldn't be able to talk until she could eat properly.

Daniela still had trouble drinking thin liquids, and her sideways tongue movement while chewing wasn't yet normal. For example, I gave her a piece of gum. After she chewed on it for several minutes and I took it out of her mouth, part of it hadn't even been chewed.

In November and December 1995, the personnel at the hospital gave Daniela everything and anything to get her to eat. Then in January, when she started eating during her hospital stay, the doctors prohibited practically everything— fats, raw fruits or vegetables, milk products, nuts, etc.

Her appetite seemed to fluctuate, and it took her a long time to eat. We became frustrated with the rigid diet the doctors prescribed. She wasn't allowed to eat cheese but was allowed to eat what we called "plastic cheese"—processed cheese slices wrapped in plastic. She wasn't supposed to eat salad because it could have a type of bacteria that was impossible to completely rinse off. We ate salad every day, and Daniela wanted some, too. She screamed when we wouldn't give it to her, so we immediately trashed the idea of prohibiting salads.

At three years and eight months of age, Alex began to ask questions like, "Can Daniela eat that?" Then he would turn to her and say, "No, Daniela, you can't have that."

Daniela often ate very little and was still receiving a quart of the baby formula through the tube. She developed candida, a fungal infection, in her mouth, and it undoubtedly hurt, so she would hardly eat anything. We also wondered if she didn't have an appetite because she was being fed through the tube. We tried reducing her formula when she began to eat more, but then she started to lose weight.

She still weighed less than she did the previous year. When she was two years old, she was in the 97th percentile for height and in the 50th percentile for weight. By six years of age, after all the chemotherapy and complications, she had dropped to the 7th percentile for height and weight. Whenever I saw her naked, she looked like a starving child from an underdeveloped country. It was heartbreaking.

Household Help (Sat., March 16, 1996)

Through our health insurance, we were able to get medical care for Daniela in the home. A nurse would come right after I had gone to work and before Joseph had to leave. If Daniela was still in bed, she woke her up, washed her, checked her temperature, changed her diaper, changed her bandage on the gastrostomy tube if needed, and got her dressed. Often, Daniela had a 'diaper blowout' as I called it, so the nurse was greeted with a big mess, which sometimes involved changing the sheets of her bed as well. Thank goodness, the pediatric nurse was used to that kind of thing. It took her about an hour and a half for Daniela's morning routine.

We were dissatisfied with some young men who had been coming into the home to look after Daniela while I went to work. They had been referred to us by home health care but were lazy and did nothing more than sit with Daniela all morning. Sometimes I would come home at lunchtime and the breakfast dishes were still on the table or Daniela was still in her pajamas, which meant that they hadn't washed her or done any of the care that she needed in the morning.

We placed an ad in the paper for household help with childcare, and the phone rang off the hook all day long. I felt like the mother in *Mrs. Doubtfire*, overwhelmed by an onslaught of unfit applicants—except this was real. Some barely spoke German, let alone English. Many were too young, and others only wanted to work two or three days a week, despite the ad specifying a daily position. Several were reluctant to earn too much for fear of paying taxes or losing unemployment benefits. Joseph and I were searching for an experienced mother and housekeeper, not a student just looking to make extra money.

Finally, we got a call from a woman who seemed perfect. Her name was Frau Selig, which means "blessed" in English—what a fitting name. She was a youthful fifty-six-year-old divorcee with one grown child. After years of working in women's clothing and shoe stores, she lost her job when the store shut down. Considered too old to be hired elsewhere, she responded to our ad. Conveniently, she lived within a five-minute bike ride from our apartment.

I initially scheduled an appointment for the next day but quickly called her back and asked if she could come that evening instead. She arrived while the kids were eating dinner, and I immediately noticed how naturally she jumped in—helping Daniela cut her food and reminding her to be careful with the knife.

By the time I returned from work that first day, Frau Selig had already folded the laundry, done some ironing, emptied the dishwasher, and cleaned the kitchen and floors. Daniela was happily playing in her room. She spent plenty of time with Daniela but took care of housework while Daniela was with a therapist.

One of the great things about living in Germany was that both the nurse's services and a large part of Frau Selig's pay were covered by our health insurance.

I still enjoyed my work, especially the flexibility. On days when I had something to take care of at home with the kids, I could go to work later, as long as I put in my four hours. On those days, Joseph picked up Alex from kindergarten.

If I left early for work, the nurse took care of Daniela, and Joseph would get Alex dressed, eat breakfast with him, and take him to kindergarten without any stress. Then he could practice at home or attend his orchestra rehearsal at 10:00 a.m.

I still hadn't been offered a permanent position at the hospital. In Germany, a job can become permanent after six months, meaning the employer could no longer fire you without just cause. Since I hadn't received an offer, I started applying for other positions within the University Hospital system. Ideally, I wanted a job that required a knowledge of the English language, as it would likely come with better pay.

To improve my pay scale, I took a typing test and far exceeded the requirements for any secretarial position—even when typing in German on a German keyboard. The Y and Z are switched because Z is used more frequently, and there are additional letters with umlauts (ö, ä, and ü). It took me a while to adjust, and for the longest time, I kept typing my name as "Tracez." But now that I'm used to the German keyboard, whenever I switch back to an American one, I find myself typing "Tracez" all over again!

In the meantime, Alex—three months shy of his fourth birthday—had entered the "why" phase. He asked "why" in response to everything, no matter what was said to him. I tried to come up with creative answers, but it could quickly become exhausting.

Since we couldn't go many places due to Daniela's risk of infection in large crowds, we had bought Alex a large Playmobil castle with knight figures for Christmas. He had always loved knights, so he was thrilled with his new Playmobil figures. He spent hours staging battles with his knights and horses, fully absorbed in his imaginary world. He even started calling himself *der blaue Ritter* ("the blue knight"). Daniela joined in, playing with the knights, too.

Once he had his castle, Alex didn't ask to watch as much TV anymore, which we saw as a good thing. With the weather warming up, we spent more time outside as well. Some days, he didn't watch any TV at all. After kindergarten, he would play with his castle until lunchtime, and then we would either go outside or take Daniela to a doctor's appointment until dinnertime. At bedtime, Joseph or I would read them a couple of children's books.

Alex was such a joy, and we were so grateful for him. He could be rough, though—he was strong and tended to hit other children. But since Joseph and I were under less stress after finding good help for Daniela, we didn't argue as much, and that seemed to have a positive effect on Alex, too.

I was amazed at how much children picked up from their parents. Whenever Alex said something, we could always tell which one of us he had learned it from. If it was in German, it had come from Joseph, since I only spoke to the kids in English.

He would say things like, *"Moment, jetzt rede ich!"* ("Wait a moment! I'm talking now!") or *"Hör jetzt zu!"* ("Now listen!")—both phrases Joseph often used with him.

Chapter 25

Relapse

In March 1996, Daniela's regular checkups and blood tests revealed that something was wrong. Fearing the worst, we took her to the hospital once again.

Frau Selig had only been working for us for two weeks when Daniela was admitted. She kindly agreed to be with Daniela at the hospital in the mornings, during the hours she would normally work at our home. She stayed with her until one of us could arrive after work.

Daniela still showed numerous symptoms of Graft vs. Host Disease. Her skin had darkened, as if she had spent a month at the beach. Her toenails had fallen off and were growing back again. The new hair that emerged was brunette instead of her usual blond, and her eyebrows had become darker and bushier. Her face was round and swollen, and her right thigh was noticeably larger than the left.

She wore a T-shirt with a photo of herself taken the previous year. On the front was a smiling, blond girl—a stark contrast to the silent Daniela sitting before me.

Her skin itched constantly, and her clothing irritated her. She tried to pull off her T-shirt—a simple task for a healthy six-year-old—but struggled to coordinate her arm movements. When her head got stuck in the shirt, she screamed in frustration.

Since the bone marrow transplant, she had been wearing diapers again. In the hospital bed, she lay in nothing but her diaper, sliding a finger under its edge to scratch her skin for hours.

One evening, Alex, Joseph, and I were visiting Daniela when I picked up our video camera and started to film her. She shook her head.

"You don't want me to film you?"

"Na," she said, covering her face with her hands and blowing a raspberry three times.

Besides saying "ah" and "nah," she had started using raspberries to protest.

She pointed toward something across the room.

"Do you want Mickey Mouse?" I asked.

"Nah," she said, still pointing.

"Do you want your doll?"

"Nah," she said, shaking her head.

"Some water?"

"Nah!" she nearly screamed, then blew another raspberry.

I felt so frustrated. I couldn't figure out what she wanted.

Letter to Family (Sun., March 24, 1996)

After two weeks on antibiotics, Daniela is still running a fever and has developed pain in her left hip and thigh. Dr. Fischer told us that on March 27, she wants to perform a bone marrow puncture. The catecholamines in Daniela's urine have also increased, which could indicate that the tumor has returned. They want to rule out a neuroblastoma, but it looks pretty bleak as far as her symptoms go. I spent all of yesterday and part of today crying.

Daniela rarely feels like doing anything anymore. She mostly stays in bed or sleeps. Over the past few days, her pain has gotten worse, and today, she couldn't even stand.

Please send us all the strength we'll need for what lies ahead.

Love, Tracey

My father called me after receiving that faxed letter.

"Maybe it's time to let her go," he said.

I didn't want to hear that.

After only about a week in the hospital, Daniela's condition was rapidly declining. She no longer got out of bed except when we put her in the stroller to take her outside to let Alex play at a nearby playground.

Sitting in the stroller outside, her eyes fluttered shut.

"Are you tired?"

"Ah," she said.

"Do you wanna sleep?"

"Ah," she said, opening and closing her eyes again.

Daniela slept a lot.

Daniela, you need a new body, I thought, my heart aching with the realization. Her body had been through so much— weakened by disease, ravaged by treatments, struggling to keep up with the spirit inside it. She was still here, still fighting, but I could see how exhausted she was. Her small frame, once full of life and energy, now seemed too fragile to contain all that she was. I wished I could take her pain away, but all I could do was sit beside her, stroke her soft, darkening hair, and hope she felt my love.

A doctor examined Daniela, gently palpitating her distended belly. She let out small noises of discomfort.

"Does that hurt?" he asked.

"Ah."

"Then I won't do it anymore."

After another round of blood tests, we met with Dr. Zimmermann to hear the results. She delivered the news as kindly as she could: Daniela's cancer had returned.

Joseph had been right—Daniela had received too much chemotherapy, enough to cause leukemia. But I had been right, too—I had wanted her to get as much as necessary to save her. And yet, despite everything—the chemotherapy, the radiation, more chemotherapy, and the bone marrow transplant—her new marrow was now filled with neuroblastoma cells. She had endured too much treatment, yet it still wasn't enough.

Dr. Zimmermann didn't need to say the words. We already knew. This was a death sentence. She had warned us before that Daniela's small body had been through more than it could bear. There was nothing left to try.

The hope we had clung to for over three and a half years shattered in an instant, vanishing as swiftly and irreversibly as a bubble bursting in the wind. We couldn't save Daniela. She was going to die. A hollow dread settled deep in my stomach, heavy and inescapable.

On March 29, 1996, Joseph and I made the decision to take Daniela home for her last days—never uttering the words "to die."

I'll Build You a Rainbow

At church, in addition to serving as a choral director, I worked with the Young Women's organization. In February and March, I had been rehearsing a song with them called "I'll Build You a Rainbow" (from "Families are Forever," with music by R. Scott Strong). Another woman from church and I had translated the lyrics and spoken text into German so we could perform it for the congregation.

It was an emotional piece—one that told the story of a young boy whose mother was fatally ill. When he asked how he would know when she was in heaven, she promised to send him a rainbow. Between the verses, the music swelled gently beneath the unfolding narrative, making the message even more heart-wrenching.

Two days before our scheduled performance, I learned that Daniela's neuroblastoma had returned. She was dying.

And yet, I still walked onto that stage and conducted that song.

When it was over, my closest girlfriends from church surrounded me. They hugged me tightly, and together, we wept.

The Last Three Weeks

The hospital sent us home with two large boxes filled with medical supplies—plasters, large 50 ml syringes for the syringe pump, glass bottles of fluids, an IV stand, and numerous prescriptions. These provisions would enable us to care for Daniela at home during her final days.

When we left the hospital for the last time, my legs felt as heavy as tree stumps. I don't even remember if I said goodbye to the nurses. In Germany, they say "*auf Wiedersehen*" ("see you again")—but we knew we wouldn't be coming back.

A home health care nurse visited daily to check on Daniela and administer her IV pain medication.

"Whoever sleeps feels no pain," Dr. Zimmermann explained. She, too, came almost every day to see Daniela.

At first, the nurse took blood samples every day. Each time, the results confirmed what we already knew—her hemoglobin was dropping as the increasing number of cancerous cells suppressed the red blood cells.

Then, one day, the nurse stopped taking blood samples. When I asked why, she answered gently, "The doctors don't think it's necessary anymore." For me, those numbers had been a kind of gauge, a way to track how close we were to the inevitable. Without them, I had nothing left to measure the time we had remaining.

I continued to prepare Daniela's liquid nutrition every day, administering it through her PEG tube.

In Germany, health insurance allowed parents to take up to ten days of leave per year to care for a sick child. (This has since been increased to fifteen days for working parents and thirty days for single working parents.) Since I had already used my allotted days, my doctor provided me with sick leave, allowing me to stay home with Daniela while still receiving my salary—one of the benefits of Germany's healthcare and social system. My employer was also understanding, for which I was truly grateful.

Both Families Visit

On April 2, my mother and my two sisters came to visit Daniela. During their one-week stay, my mother-in-law and sister-in-law also traveled from Bavaria for a couple of days. It was the first—and only—time these two sides of our family met. Olivia had learned a little bit of German and did her best to communicate with my mother-in-law, who spoke no English. My sister-in-law knew a little English from secondary school, but not enough for more than a few phrases. They all smiled politely at each other, laughing at jokes or comments they didn't fully understand.

On Easter Sunday, my mother-in-law made her delicious apple strudel for everyone. Joseph went on an outing to St. Peter in the Black Forest with his mother, sister, Alex, our friend

Jakob, and Jakob's son. Meanwhile, my mom and sisters stayed at home with me and Daniela. Everyone acted as though things were normal. I found that both comforting and disorienting.

By this point, Daniela began to develop mouth sores. Her lower lip was swollen and chapped. During that final week, she slept on the double-sized couch bed in our office. Sometimes Alex would choose to sleep beside her.

I don't know what compelled me to tell Daniela the truth. Maybe it was just my nature—always open and honest. I told her she was going to die. She thrashed in protest and cried, "Na, na, na!"

Inside, I felt the same. My heart ached.

The Last Day (Mon., April 15, 1996)

Tanja—Daniela's friend from church who went with us to Mallorca—asked her mom if she could visit Daniela. Her mom called me to relay their conversation.

"I want to see Daniela today," Tanja said.

"Does it have to be today?" her mom asked.

"Yes. It has to be today."

"But it's getting late. Can't we wait until tomorrow?"

"No," Tanja insisted.

"Well, I'll call Tracey and see if it's not too late."

When I heard that Tanja had asked to come, I said, "Then she should see her."

That afternoon, Tanja stood quietly beside Daniela's bed, gently stroking her arm.

While some parents might shield young children from death, the Mormons were not afraid to expose their children to it early on. They believe we will be reunited with loved ones who have gone before us.

As it turned out, Tanja was Daniela's last visitor.

The Last Hours

Daniela had been restless all evening. Joseph sensed that the end was near.

"This is going to be some night," he said.

It grew late, and Daniela was still moving in her sleep, as if in pain. We added painkillers to her PEG, but they didn't seem to help.

I called Dr. Zimmermann. She was at a dinner party but said it was no problem—she'd come right over.

She arrived after 11:00 p.m., examined Daniela, and agreed she needed something stronger.

"I have some morphine in the car," she said.

"Are you sure? Didn't she have a bad reaction the last time we gave it to her?"

"I think her immune system is so weakened now that she likely won't react to it," she replied.

Dr. Zimmermann returned from her car and injected Daniela's central line with morphine.

It didn't take long before Daniela began to calm down, though her breathing remained fast and shallow. She was lying on the couch bed in our office. Dr. Zimmermann, Joseph, and I surrounded her. Alex joined us. I don't remember why he was still awake, but somehow it felt right that he was.

Shortly after midnight, I sat watching Daniela's chest rise and fall with her quick, labored breaths. Suddenly, I felt a sensation that was impossible to describe—something I had never felt before or since. It was like a surge of energy—a strong vibration rushing through my solar plexus and abdomen. It lasted only a second.

"What was that?" I asked out loud, startled by the intensity of it.

I looked at Daniela and noticed that her chest movement had stopped.

"She's stopped breathing," I whispered. I stared down at her. She lay completely still. "I think she's leaving us."

Then I understood what I had experienced. Without a doubt, what I had just felt was Daniela's spirit leaving her body. She had passed through me on her way out of this world—and I had felt it!

I looked up at the clock on the wall. It was two minutes past midnight on April 16, 1996.

To this day, I carry with me the absolute assurance that our spirit lives on after death. If energy cannot be created nor destroyed, then surely our spirit—our essence—is a form of energy that is simply transformed.

I felt my daughter's spirit pass through me as she left this life. That moment is a sacred gift that no one can take from me.

When I later told Joseph what I had felt, I asked if he had experienced anything.

"I didn't feel anything," he said, "but I saw something float up through the ceiling."

Even Alex must have observed something. Not long after Daniela's death, he sat down at our desk in the office and began to draw with a pencil.

"What are you drawing, Alex?" I asked.

"*Daniela als Engel*," he replied—Daniela as an angel—completely absorbed in his work.

The drawing looked as though Alex, too, had witnessed something beyond this world. Lines radiated outward from the stick figure, as if to show an aura or spirit, and there appeared to be a cross in the center of the body. He was just one month shy of his fourth birthday when he lost his sister.

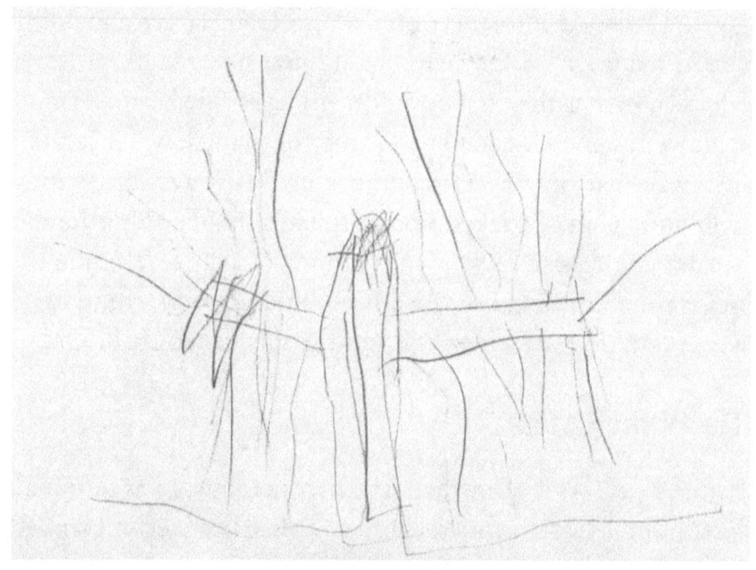

"Daniela als Engel" ("Daniela as an Angel")

A Mother's Cry

I think Joseph stayed awake most of the night to be with Daniela. I went to bed, though I don't remember sleeping.

Early the next morning, the birds were chirping—as if nothing had changed.

At least you chose a beautiful day to die, Daniela.

But *everything* had changed. That day passed in a blur as people came and went, paying their last respects. A girlfriend from church showed up at our door with her daughter, who was about Daniela's age. She had come expecting to visit, unaware of what had happened. When I opened the door dressed in black, she understood immediately. She gave me a long, silent hug.

I remember not shedding a single tear while friends came to visit. I kept my sorrow tucked away, wearing the quiet mask of strength—until around 5:00 p.m., when the last guest had gone. I stepped into the room where Daniela lay and softly closed the door behind me. The stillness met me like a wave. I looked at her lifeless body, and my eyes filled with tears. I sank to my knees beside her, letting the tears flow. I cried out in a way that only a mother can know—in raw, unrelenting pain and agony. I sobbed uncontrollably, not caring if Joseph or Alex could hear. I was alone with my daughter, releasing the weight of all the anguish I had been holding back—until there were no more tears left to cry, and the silence returned.

The White Coffin

Before Daniela's death, when we knew her illness was terminal, Joseph and I visited a funeral home that had been recommended to us. It was run by a woman in her fifties who spoke with gentle kindness, her voice soft and caring as she helped us choose a coffin. It was made of oak, stained white, with six sides—tapered at the head and foot, and wide at the shoulders. And it was child sized.

In the United States, a body is placed on a stretcher, covered, and transported by ambulance, hearse, or minivan. In Germany, the body is placed directly in a coffin before being taken to the hearse.

Around 6:00 p.m., we had arranged for the funeral service to pick up Daniela. When Alex saw two men enter our apartment carrying a small white coffin, he screamed, *"Tür zu! Tür zu!"* ("Close the door! Close the door!").

He ran to our office and shut the door, standing in front of it to block the men from coming in. Joseph quietly led them through the living room and out onto the balcony, which had a second door to the office. They carried the coffin in that way to reach Daniela.

I spent the rest of the time trying to comfort Alex.

When we visited Daniela at the funeral home, it felt really cold inside—like a big refrigerator. The air was heavy with the sharp scent of disinfectant or some other chemical I couldn't quite place. It was a smell I know I'll recognize instantly if I ever encounter it again.

Daniela was laid out for us on a table in one of the rooms. The sight unsettled me. I didn't like that she had to remain there for nearly a week until the funeral the following Monday. We didn't want to hold the service on Friday, hoping to give family from Bavaria enough time to make travel arrangements. Since funerals weren't held over the weekend, we settled on Monday.

I wore black every day until the funeral. It wasn't until after Daniela was laid to rest that I felt a small sense of peace. After that, I stopped wearing black, though I continued to dress in dark, muted colors for several weeks, a quiet reflection of my mood.

Many people attended the funeral: friends from church, doctors and nurses, and family from Bavaria. Our dear friend Jakob gave a eulogy, as did Joseph. An American friend of mine, a professional opera singer, sang "Shall We Gather at the River" a cappella. It was achingly beautiful. She told me later it was one of the hardest performances of her life—holding her composure while singing for people she cared so deeply about. A string quartet from Joseph's orchestra played at the gravesite. Angelina was there, too.

During the service, the clouds parted, and sunlight streamed through the stained-glass window high above, casting a warm, colorful light into the otherwise somber room. Joseph and I both felt Daniela's presence in that moment—as though she had come to be with us. Afterward, when we spoke with Angelina, we asked her about the light. She gently confirmed what we already sensed: Daniela's spirit had been close by.

Chapter 26

Aftermath

Two weeks after the funeral, I jolted awake, panicked that I had forgotten to mix Daniela's nutrition and load it into her syringe pump—until the weight of reality hit me.

A recurring dream began to haunt me—some version of discovering that Daniela was still alive, living in an institution just hours away. After those dreams, I would feel unsettled all day, carrying a nagging sense that I had abandoned her, left her in the care of strangers.

Even now, years later, dreams of Daniela come unexpectedly. In them, she is alive and well—skipping, laughing, talking. I think what hurt most was that she couldn't speak for the last ten months of her life.

It wasn't until after she died that I realized I had lost her twice. I mourned the speechless, dark-skinned, dark-haired girl whose body had been changed beyond recognition—transformed by illness and treatment, silenced by the complications of chemotherapy.

I also grieved the blond, spirited child I had known before—the one who sang, danced, and filled our home with chatter.

I think that was why the grieving was especially difficult: Until the very end, I held on to the hope that the healthy Daniela would return. But she never did.

I often think about the fight we had over the cheap doll I had refused to buy her. The memory still brings tears. If I could turn back time, I would have bought her that doll—and anything else she wanted—knowing she didn't have much time left to enjoy her childhood.

We parents worry about spoiling our children, about teaching them life's limits. But what was I trying to teach her? That you can't always get what you want? The one thing I wanted most was for my daughter to get well. And I learned, in the most painful way, that I couldn't have that.

Daniela's courage—her will to live—moved everyone who knew her. After her death, my father tried to comfort me, "We're grateful she was with us for six years," he said.

I accepted his condolences in silence. But inside, I was screaming, *It's not enough! I wanted more. I wanted to watch her grow up, fall in love, raise children of her own.*

Even now, I wonder who Daniela might have become. But I am truly grateful for the time we had. I didn't want her life—or her experience—to be forgotten. That's why I wrote this memoir.

I may never understand why her life was so short, or why we had to endure such loss. But it comforts me to believe that when I die, I'll be reunited with her. Or perhaps a part of her higher self has been reincarnated into another child—one who can finally live a long, full, joyful life.

She deserves that.

Every child deserves that.

Epilogue

Time heals all.

Does it really? I think the passage of time serves to lessen the pain.

We had to get used to living without Daniela. About six months after her death, Joseph, Alex, and I were visiting friends from church.

"What time do your kids go to bed?" I asked.

After she answered, I said, "Ours go to bed around 8:00 or 8:30 p.m."

Then I caught myself.

"I mean, our child—Alex—goes to bed…"

My voice trailed off.

Even half a year later, I wasn't used to saying I had only one child.

That summer, Joseph and I took Alex to a playground. I saw siblings laughing and playing together, and it hit me like a wave—I wanted Alex to have a brother or sister again.

That night I turned to Joseph and said, "I want another child."

"I do, too," he replied.

By September, I was expecting. Since I had lost my right fallopian tube during the tubal pregnancy, it felt like a small miracle that I had ovulated on the left side during the very first month we tried. Matt was born the following June, just fourteen months after Daniela's death. I was thirty-seven years old.

Right after Matt's birth, while I was still in the hospital, I was flooded with anxiety. My heart raced. I didn't want Joseph and Alex to leave. I overheard Joseph quietly explaining to the nurse, "We lost our daughter last year." Eventually, I calmed down enough to let them go.

Fifteen months after Daniela died, Alex—then five—sat down to watch *The Lion King*. Before the movie began, the video showed a preview of *The Aristocats,* with the song *Everybody Wants to be a Cat*—the tune Daniela and Alex used to sing and dance to together. As soon as I heard it, I broke down and retreated to the bathroom to cry. I missed her so much. But I also cried for Alex, who no longer had his big sister.

Years later, a friend approached me and said, "I was cleaning out a drawer and found this photo of Daniela. I thought you might like to have it."

It showed her daughter and Daniela seated in a horse and buggy at Europa Park. I had never seen it before. Daniela looked so happy. It made me cry.

Another time, I was visiting a friend when her teenage daughter came into the room in tears. Whatever had happened, she ran straight to her mother for comfort. Watching that simple moment brought tears to my eyes. I realized I would never experience that with Daniela—never see her become a teenager and come crying to me.

When Matt was in kindergarten, one of his teachers pulled me aside.

"I'm a little concerned. Matt keeps telling us he had a sister who passed away."

"What he's saying is true," I told her.

Matt was born after Daniela died. He never knew her, yet he spoke about her as if he had. He'd only seen her in family photos on our wall.

I like to think Matt knew Daniela on a higher level.

Even years later, small events can trigger me unexpectedly.

In 2004, eight years after Daniela died, Joseph and I visited an art exhibit at the Augustiner Museum in Freiburg. By then, Alex was twelve and Matt was seven. I walked up the wide staircase to the second floor and found myself facing a large oil painting: *Drei Kinder der Familie Schinzinger* ("Three Children of the Schinzinger Family") by Adolf Schmidlin (1868–1954).

It showed two boys and a blond girl lounging on a grassy hill overlooking Freiburg. The boys wore matching blue outfits, and the girl—dressed in white—sat between them.

It was like seeing my own children. The boys reminded me of Alex and Matt. And the girl, with her white dress and golden hair, could have been Daniela. It was as if I were seeing Daniela as an angel with my two sons.

Suddenly, it struck me: I would never have a picture of all three of my children together. Ever. I cried right there in the museum, unable to stop the tears.

I took home a poster of the painting, which I framed and hung on the wall. It has stayed there ever since—a symbol of my three children, who never lived together at the same time.

While writing this memoir, I reached out to the museum. I told them about losing my daughter, about how much that painting meant to me, and asked—somewhat boldly—whether

I could purchase the original. I had no idea what it would cost, but I knew it was no longer on display and had been catalogued and placed in storage.

I received a very kind email sharing their condolences but stating that they couldn't sell the piece. Instead, they generously attached a high-quality digital image. I used that file to order a large, beautifully framed print to replace the old poster.

That print now hangs on my wall—a quiet tribute to my three children, a reminder of what we lost and what we still hold close.

Acknowledgements

I would like to extend my deepest gratitude to all the doctors, nurses, therapists, and staff involved in Daniela's care. While many of you are referred to more generally throughout this memoir—such as "the nurse" or "the night nurse"—your dedication remains vivid in my memory. I truly appreciate each one of you who has devoted your life's work to helping sick children.

I am also immensely thankful for the unwavering support of our friends from the Church of Jesus Christ of Latter-day Saints. Although I've condensed your contributions into one or two characters, many of you provided invaluable help—whether by bringing us meals in the ICU, or by caring for Daniela or her baby brother when we couldn't be there. Your generosity and kindness will never be forgotten.

I am deeply grateful to Aristhaia Cash, whose gracious support brought healing and hope throughout our journey.

Special thanks to Padumachitta Goch for reading an early draft of this manuscript and offering encouragement when it was most needed.

Heartfelt thanks to Prof. Dr. Klaus-Dieter Rückauer for reviewing the manuscript for medical accuracy and providing valuable feedback.

Finally, my heartfelt appreciation goes to the remarkable head physician behind "Dr. Zimmermann." Her blend of professionalism and compassion brought me immeasurable comfort and hope—not only during our most difficult moments, but throughout the entire journey. I will always be grateful for the care and humanity she showed not only to Daniela but to me as a mother.

References

Bombeck, Erma. "*I Want to Grow Hair, I Want to Grow Up, I Want to Go to Boise.*" Harper Collins, 1989.

Katharinenhöhe Family Rehab Center. https://www.katharinenhoehe.de

Eadie, Betty J. "*Embraced by the Light: What Happens When You Die.*" Gold Leaf Press, 1992.

Radner, Gilda. "*It's Always Something.*" Simon and Schuster, 1989.

Siegel, Bernie S., M.D. "*Love, Medicine and Miracles: Lessons Learned About Self-Healing from a Surgeon's Experience with Exceptional Patients.*" Harper Perennial, 1988.

Förderverein für Krebskranke Kinder e.V. Freiburg (Support Association for Children with Cancer Freiburg). www.helfen-hilft.de

Georgian, Linda. "*Your Guardian Angels: Use the Power of Angelic Messengers to Enrich and Empower Your Life.*" Touchstone, 1994.

Strong, R. Scott. "*I'll Build You a Rainbow.*" From *Families are Forever*, music by R. Scott Strong.

Schmidlin, Adolf. "*Drei Kinder der Familie Schinzinger, 1909–10.*" Öl auf Leinwand ("*Three Children of the Schinzinger Family,*" oil on canvas). Inv. Nr. 1995/304, Augustinermuseum, Freiburg i. Br. Permalink: https://onlinesammlung.freiburg.de/de/object/206FA75E48E44F489A5366BD8EE4379D

About the Author

Tracey Ann Webb was born in Miami, Florida, and spent her teenage years in the scenic Blue Ridge Mountains of North Georgia. She earned a Master of Music degree from the New England Conservatory in Boston. After studying and living in several cities across Germany, she settled in Freiburg in 1989.

Although Tracey began writing at an early age, she paused her creative pursuits for many years to focus on family and career. In 2010, she returned to writing, contributing lyrics to albums for the Cécile Verny Quartet, a professional jazz ensemble based in Freiburg, Germany. This collaboration reignited her passion for poetry and storytelling.

Through her writing, Tracey seeks to connect with readers on a deeply emotional level, sharing stories that explore love, suffering, and the beauty of human connection.

Today, Tracey leads amateur pop choirs in the Freiburg region and continues to compose and arrange music. She is the mother of three children and shares her home with Katniss, a sweet tabby cat who charms every visitor.

Blue Mittens is her first book, inspired by her experiences as a mother.

www.ingramcontent.com/pod-product-compliance
Lightning Source LLC
Chambersburg PA
CBHW032016150726
47990CB00005B/1990